D0066092

"James Bryan Smith rightly understands that to be a Christian is not so much a conferred status as it is a journey we embark upon—a journey toward Christlikeness. This journey of apprenticeship is less about learning right beliefs and more about employing right practices. If we are to make progress in Christlikeness, we need what Smith calls 'soul training.' And this is what makes *The Magnificent Journey* such an exciting and valuable book. With *The Magnificent Journey* James Bryan Smith blazes a trail for all who desire to live deep in the kingdom of Christ."

Brian Zahnd, pastor of Word of Life Church, St. Joseph, Missouri, and author of *Sinners In the Hands of a Loving God*

"Spiritual formation writers and spiritual directors have shifted from the spiritual disciplines to story and narrative and to journey, and the leading light on this reconfiguration of spiritual formation is James Bryan Smith. In *The Magnificent Journey* you will be embraced by the story of the kingdom of God, a story that leads us into faith, hope, love, and—best of all—joy. This book, when accompanied by the grace of God's Spirit, can guide churches into that surprise called joy."

Scot McKnight, professor of New Testament, Northern Seminary

"With the depth of a scholar and the posture of a friend, James Bryan Smith offers profound truth we are desperate to remember: God is near, Jesus is with us, and his kingdom remains strong and unshakable. If you're looking for the kind of truth that actually makes a difference in your life, this book is a must-read."

Emily P. Freeman, author of *Simply Tuesday*

"I am grateful to God for Jim and for this wonderful guide to kingdom life. It offers beauty and wisdom and power."

John Ortberg, senior pastor, Menlo Church, and author of *I'd Like You More If You Were More Like Me*

"Too often our thinking about growing as followers of Jesus is focused on our own activities for God. But God invites us to cultivate humble receptivity which would then give birth to holy activity. Obedience is then a response to grace. Surrender is then a response to love. Smith speaks here from lived wisdom about the transforming privilege of loving abandon to divine generosity. I highly recommend this book."
Alan Fadling, author of *An Unhurried Life* and *An Unhurried Leader*

"Deep and accessible, profound and personal, James Bryan Smith offers the very best writing in spiritual transformation. He's the ideal guide for this magnificent journey. Walk with him and you will become the good and beautiful *you* that God created you to be."
Ken Shigematsu, pastor of Tenth Church, Vancouver, BC, and author of *Survival Guide for the Soul*

"In *The Magnificent Journey*, James Bryan Smith masterfully pulls from different voices and movements in the Christian tradition to chart the way of Jesus. His writing is conversational and full of great stories even as he speaks of the ineffable. He is able to hold at once mysticism and down-to-earth practicality. Most critically, he casts a vision of life that makes me long to know Jesus more."
Tish Harrison Warren, author of *Liturgy of the Ordinary*, and priest in the Anglican Church of North America

THE *Magnificent* JOURNEY

Living Deep
in the Kingdom

JAMES BRYAN SMITH

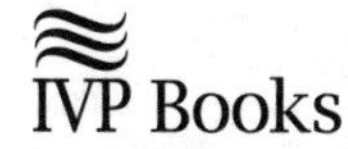

An imprint of InterVarsity Press
Downers Grove, Illinois

InterVarsity Press
P.O. Box 1400, Downers Grove, IL 60515-1426
ivpress.com
email@ivpress.com

InterVarsity Press® is the book-publishing division of InterVarsity Christian Fellowship/USA®, a movement of students and faculty active on campus at hundreds of universities, colleges, and schools of nursing in the United States of America, and a member movement of the International Fellowship of Evangelical Students. For information about local and regional activities, visit intervarsity.org.

While any stories in this book are true, some names and identifying information may have been changed to protect the privacy of individuals.

The Annunciation, 1898, by Henry Ossawa Tanner (1859–1937). Philadelphia Museum of Art, Pennsylvania, PA, USA. Purchased with the W. P. Wilstach Fund, 1899/Bridgeman Images. Used by permission.

The Ecstasy of St. Theresa, 1652, by Gianlorenzo Bernini. Photo by Jastrow, 2006, https://commons.wikimedia.org/w/index.php?curid=1290870.

Cover design: Cindy Kiple
Interior design: Jeanna Wiggins
Images: Tree of Life by Gustav Klimt at MAK (Austrian Museum of Applied Arts) Vienna, Austria/De Agostini Picture Library/Bridgeman Images

ISBN 978-0-8308-4638-2 (print)
ISBN 978-0-8308-8929-7 (digital)

Printed in Canada ♾

InterVarsity Press is committed to ecological stewardship and to the conservation of natural resources in all our operations. This book was printed using sustainably sourced paper.

Library of Congress Cataloging-in-Publication Data

Names: Smith, James Bryan, author.
Title: The magnificent journey : living deep in the kingdom / James Bryan Smith.
Description: Downers Grove : InterVarsity Press, 2018. | Series: Apprentice resources | Includes bibliographical references and index.
Identifiers: LCCN 2018028450 (print) | LCCN 2018034438 (ebook) | ISBN 9780830889297 (eBook) | ISBN 9780830846382 (hardcover : alk. paper)
Subjects: LCSH: Spiritual life—Christianity. | Spiritual formation. | Christian life.
Classification: LCC BV4501.3 (ebook) | LCC BV4501.3 .S65243 2018 (print) | DDC 248.4—dc23
LC record available at https://lccn.loc.gov/2018028450

P 21 20 19 18 17 16 15 14 13 12 11 10 9 8 7 6 5 4 3 2 1
Y 35 34 33 32 31 30 29 28 27 26 25 24 23 22 21 20 19 18

To Dallas Willard,

who invited me and guided me on this

magnificent journey of eternal living,

without whom I would not

have known it existed

Contents

How to Get the Most Out of This Book

This book is intended to be used in the context of a community—a small group, a Sunday school class, or a few friends gathered in a home or coffee shop. Working through this book with others greatly magnifies the impact. If you go through this on your own, only the first four of the following suggestions will apply to you. No matter how you use it, I am confident that God can and will accomplish a good work in you.

1. *Prepare*: Find a notebook or journal with blank pages. You will use this journal to answer questions sprinkled throughout each chapter (in boxes) and for reflecting on the soul training exercises (instructions are at the end of each chapter).

2. *Read*: Read each chapter thoroughly. Try not to read hurriedly, and avoid reading the chapter at the last minute. Start reading early enough in the week so you have time to digest the material and to do the exercise.

3. *Do*: Complete the weekly soul training exercise. Engaging in exercises related to the content of the chapter will help deepen the ideas and narratives you will be learning. It can also be

healing, as it connects you to God. The exercises in this book are best done over several days.

4. *Reflect*: Make time to complete your written reflections. You may not be a journaling type, but I encourage you to find some way to keep track of your answers to the box questions as well as your reflections on the exercise.
5. *Interact*: Come to the group prepared to listen and share. If everyone takes time to write out answers in advance, the group conversation will be much richer, and your time together will be more effective. Remember the group discussion rule: listen twice as much as you speak. But do speak! The other group members will learn from your ideas and experiences.
6. *Encourage*: Interact with each other outside of group time. Use technology to stay in touch with the members of your group between gatherings. One good idea is to have a group email thread in which someone posts a thought or idea or question, and others can chime in. Another great thing to do is intentionally email at least one person in your group each week with an encouraging word.

Part One

Living Deep in the Kingdom

1

The Way of Surrender

Two roads diverged in a wood, and I—
I took the one less traveled by,
And that has made all the difference.

Robert Frost

During my second year of seminary, the spiritual moorings of my life came loose. I had been studying *about* God but had grown distant *from* God. I decided to go on a five-day silent retreat at an Episcopalian monastery in the Northeast to try to reclaim the spiritual warmth I had somehow lost.

Upon arrival I was assigned a monk who would be my spiritual director for one hour each day. He walked into our meeting room with jogging clothes underneath his cowl. I was disappointed. I had been expecting an elderly man, bearded to his knees, who would penetrate my soul with searing blue eyes. Instead, I got "the jogging monk."

My director gave me only one task for the day: meditate on the story of the Annunciation in the first chapter of Luke's Gospel. I walked back to my room wondering how I would occupy my time with only this one assignment. *After all,* I thought to myself, *I could exegete this entire text in a few hours.*

What was I to do for the rest of the day—in silence?

Back at my room I opened my Bible to the passage and began reading. "Birth narrative," I muttered to myself. For the next hour I spliced and diced the verses as any good exegete would do, ending up with a few hypotheses and several hours to sit in silence. As the hours passed the room seemed to get smaller. There was no view to the outside through the window of my room. Other rooms, I would come to find, had a beautiful view of the river that flowed adjacent to the monastery. Without any view to the outer world, I was forced to look within. Despite my hopes of finding spiritual bliss, I had never felt more alone.

Why is it often difficult for us to look within? What are we afraid we will find?

The next day I met with the monk again to discuss my spiritual life. He asked what had happened with the assigned text. I told him it was just shy of disaster in terms of profound spiritual revelations, but that I had come up with a few exegetical insights. I thought my discoveries might impress him.

They didn't.

"What was your aim in reading this passage?" he asked.

"My aim? To arrive at an understanding of the meaning of the text, I suppose."

"Anything else?"

I paused. "No. What else is there?"

"Well, there's more than just finding out what it says and what it means. There are also questions like, What did it teach you? What did it say to you? Were you struck by anything? And most important, Did you experience God in your reading?"

He assigned the same text for the next day, asking me to begin reading it not so much with my head but more with my heart.

I had no idea how to do this. For the first three hours I tried and failed repeatedly. I practically had the passage memorized, and still it was lifeless and I was bored. The room seemed even smaller, and by nightfall, I thought I would go deaf from the silence.

The next day we met again. In despair I told him that I simply could not do what he was asking me to do. It was then that the wisdom beneath the jogging clothes became evident.

"You're trying too hard, Jim. You're trying to control God. You're running the show. Go back and read this passage again.

"But this time, be open to receive whatever God has for you. Don't manipulate God; just receive. Communion with him isn't something you institute. It's like sleep. You can't make yourself sleep, but you can create the conditions that allow sleep to happen. All I want you to do is create the conditions: open your Bible, read it slowly, listen to it, and reflect on it."

I went back to my room (it had a prisonlike feel by now) and began to read. I found utter silence. After an hour I finally shouted, "I give up! You win!" (though I am not certain who I was shouting at). I slumped over in my chair and began to weep. I suspect that God had been waiting for me to let go.

A short time later I picked up the Bible and read the passage again. The words looked different, despite their familiarity. My mind and heart were supple as I read. I was no longer trying to figure out the meaning or the main point of the passage. I was simply hearing it.

My eyes fell upon the well-loved words of Mary, "Let it be with me according to your word," her response to God's stunning promise that she would give birth to his Son. *Let it be with me.* The words rang in my head. And then God spoke to me. Some might say it was "all in my head" or "just my imagination," but how else does God speak?

It was as if a window had been thrown open and God was suddenly present, like a friend who wanted to talk. What followed was a dialogue about the story in Luke, about God, about Mary, and about me. I wondered about Mary—her feelings, her doubts, her fears, and her incredible willingness to respond to God's request.

This prompted me to ask (or the Spirit moved me to ask) about the limits of my obedience, which seemed meager in comparison to Mary's. "Do not be afraid," said the angel to Mary. We talked about fear. What was I afraid of? What held me back?

"You have found favor with God," the angel told Mary. Had I found favor with God? I sensed that I had, but not because of anything I had done (humility had become my companion in that room). I had found favor because I was his child.

I wondered too about the future, about my calling. What did God want of me? Mary had just been informed of her destiny. What was mine? We talked about what might be—what, in fact, could be if I were willing. If I were willing. Like Augustine, who turned to the Scriptures after hearing a voice say, "Take up and read," I had reached the end of my rope and was, for the first time in a long time, in a position to hear. There is much to be said for desperation, as desperation led me to begin praying. My prayer was really a plea: Help me. After an hour of reflecting and listening, Mary's "Let it be with me according to your word" eventually became my prayer. The struggle had ended. I had a feeling that I had just lost control of my life but in that same moment had finally found my life.

The room that had seemed small now seemed spacious. The fact that there was no view no longer mattered. The view was wonderful from my vantage point. The silence no longer mattered, no longer made me anxious. Now it seemed peaceful. And the terrible feeling of being alone was replaced by a sense of closeness with a God who was, in the words of St. Augustine, "nearer to me than I was to myself."

LET IT BE

My favorite painting is *The Annunciation* by Henry Ossawa Tanner. It is based on Luke 1:26-38, wherein the angel Gabriel announces to Mary that she will give birth to a Son who will save the world.

An African American, Tanner (1859–1937) was the son of a minister in the African Methodist Episcopal Church. Tanner grew up

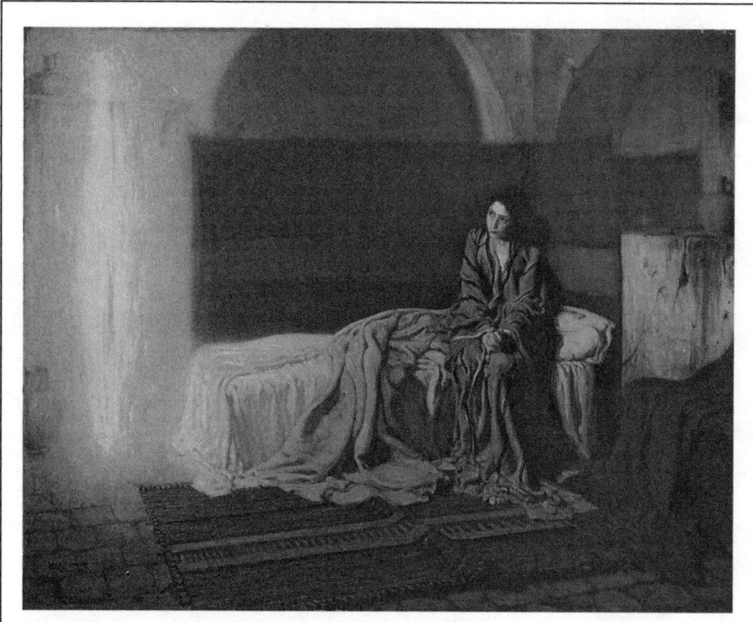

The Annunciation by Henry Ossawa Tanner, 1898

with a deep love and knowledge of the Bible. He also knew firsthand the challenge of living as a Christian in a world of racial hatred and discrimination. He spent the latter half of his life in Paris where he found less discrimination.

Tanner painted *The Annunciation* when he returned to Paris from a trip to Egypt and Palestine in 1897. On that trip he wanted to see the Holy Land so his painting could be more realistic. Nearly every painting of Mary, particularly of the Annunciation, depicts Mary as wealthy, dressed in expensive, beautiful gowns, with a serene look on her face and a halo above her to show her sanctity. And often the architecture around her is grand. In Tanner's painting, Mary looks like an adolescent dressed in simple peasant's clothing, in a simple peasant home. It is as if she is about to wake up in her bed with a rumpled bedspread. If you look closely you can even see her toes poking out of the blanket.

In most Annunciation paintings, Gabriel is depicted as a winged creature of power. Tanner depicts Gabriel as a shaft of light. The light coming from Gabriel floods the room (notice the shadows), making the face of Mary the center of the painting. And it is the face of Mary that I most love. It is the perfect combination of fear and faith, of anxiety and submission. Many Annunciation paintings have Mary reading or praying or working, thus showing her piety and intellect and industriousness. Not here. Here Mary is doing nothing, as far as we can tell.

How did you first react when you saw Tanner's The Annunciation*? Do you appreciate its realism, or do you find it off-putting?*

I love this painting because it is simple and ordinary. As Scott Lamb notes, "Tanner depicts Mary in a moment of peaceful submission to the will of God. But even in this, Mary looks normal in the sense that we too could follow God's will for our own lives even as she did."

Long before the Beatles sang these words of wisdom, Mary responded to Gabriel by saying, "Let it be with me . . ." Let it be. I accept. These are words of obedience and surrender. It is a declaration of acceptance of God's will. It is an offering of her will and her life to God. It is in keeping with words her son would proclaim many years later when he taught about the narrow gate. It is the gate through which our magnificent journey into deep kingdom living begins.

THE NARROW GATE

The "let it be with me" movement of surrender is the starting point and the entrance requirement of the magnificent journey. It is a posture of obedience. To surrender and obey is the gateway to living deep in the kingdom of God. The Sermon on the Mount (Matthew 5–7) is the greatest teaching ever given, by the greatest teacher who ever lived: Jesus. The central verse of the sermon is Matthew 6:33: "Strive first for the kingdom of God and his righteousness, and all these things will be given to you as well." To seek first the kingdom is to desire to do God's will and to live in God's way. When we do this, we are living interactively with the power, provision, and protection of the kingdom of God.

> *The "let it be with me" movement of surrender is the starting point and the entrance requirement of the magnificent journey.*

Later in this great sermon, Jesus tells his listeners, "Enter through the narrow gate; for the gate is wide and the road is easy that leads to destruction, and there are many who take it. For the gate is narrow and the road is hard that leads to life, and there are few who find it" (Matthew 7:13-14). The narrow gate is a metaphor for choosing to obey the teaching of Jesus in the sermon. It is choosing to go the second mile, to give rather than receive, not to be angry with your brother or sister, to bless those who curse you, to forgive one another, and not to judge or worry.

As one commentator noted, "Jesus himself is the narrow gate through which people pass as they respond to his invitation to the kingdom of heaven. The way of discipleship then stretches throughout one's years on earth, ultimately leading to life eternal." Stepping through the narrow gate is choosing to live as Jesus' apprentice, to seek to obey everything he teaches. If you stop and think about the kinds of things required as Jesus' apprentice (stated earlier), you can see the truth of Jesus' words: "There are few who find it." It is sad but true. The majority of people are not blessing those who curse them, much less even trying to do so. Though my assessment may seem harsh, this is also true of many Christians. Some have speculated that only 10 percent of a given congregation actually intend to obey these kinds of commands. I work a lot with pastors, and when I have shared that percentage with them, the most common response is, "Jim, I think that number is a bit high."

Stepping through the narrow gate is choosing to live as Jesus' apprentice, to seek to obey everything he teaches.

THE ROAD LESS TRAVELED

Choosing to live in obedience to Jesus and his teaching is, as Robert Frost put it, a road "less traveled by." The road more traveled is the one Jesus spoke about, where "the gate is wide and the road is easy that leads to destruction, and there are many who take it" (Matthew 7:13). Jesus is not being mean, he is being honest. As human beings we are naturally drawn to that which is easy. Due to the Fall, we are also living in a darkened world with darkened minds. We feel isolated and alone, afraid and anxious, and the world we live in preaches, "Look out for yourself first," "Greed is good," and "Nice guys finish last." They are roads more traveled.

But they do not lead to a magnificent journey.

The road of self-absorption leads to a paltry journey at best, and at worst they are the way to destruction and ruin. Surrender and obedience to Jesus is difficult. To die to oneself, to take up one's cross, is a "hard" road but one that "leads to life." Unfortunately, "there are few who find it." There are many reasons why people do not find it. In addition to it being difficult, it is also a road too few Christians even hear about. Dallas Willard often said he never attended a church that had a well-designed, intently pursued *plan* for making disciples of Jesus. It is often untried because it is unknown.

But it is the way to life.

We cannot enter into the kingdom unless we take up the cross. The cross leads to the magnificent journey of living in the unshakable kingdom of God. It is the unavoidable prerequisite. Again, to quote Willard, "Christian spiritual formation rests on this indispensable foundation of death to self and cannot proceed except insofar as that foundation is being firmly laid and sustained." We often assume that dying to self will be painful. And of course it is. But what is the alternative? Søren Kierkegaard called the failure to do this "a sickness unto death." Humanity, he believed, lives in a kind of despair until it finds its rest in the One who made it. This is similar to the penetrating insight of St. Augustine: "Thou hast made us for Thyself, O God, and our hearts are restless until they find their rest in Thee."

I can, for example, choose to navigate my life, live as I want, and aim at fulfilling all of my desires. This will result in that despair Kierkegaard wrote of, the sickness unto death. Willard called this a "dying self." The wisest, best choice, then, is "the surrender of a lesser, dying self for a greater eternal one." Or to quote the martyred missionary Jim Elliot, "He is no fool who gives what he cannot keep to gain that which he cannot lose."

Formation in Christlikeness depends on surrender; failure to surrender is a sickness unto death; I can never find rest until I surrender; I am exchanging a lesser for a greater; and giving what I cannot keep in exchange for what I cannot lose is wise, not foolish. Deep reflection on these realities goes a long way toward helping me choose to take up my cross and die to myself.

THE COST OF NONDISCIPLESHIP

Dietrich Bonhoeffer wrote a masterful book titled *The Cost of Discipleship*. In it he attacks the "cheap grace" he sees so often among Christians who ask everything from God and are willing to offer nothing in return. It is true that the cost of discipleship is steep, but it is also true that the cost of *non*discipleship is even higher. In one of my favorite Dallas Willard quotes, he beautifully describes what is lost when we choose *not* to surrender to Jesus, not to live as his apprentice:

> *What have you seen in your life as the cost of nondiscipleship?*

> Nondiscipleship costs abiding peace, a life penetrated throughout by love, faith that sees everything in the light of God's overriding governance for good, hopefulness that stands firm in the most discouraging of circumstances, power to do what is right and withstand the forces of evil. In short,

> it costs exactly that abundance of life Jesus said he came to bring (John 10:10). The cross-shaped yoke of Christ is after all an instrument of liberation and power to those who live in it with him and learn the meekness and lowliness of heart that brings rest to the soul. . . . The correct perspective is to see following Christ not only as the necessity it is, but as the fulfillment of the highest human possibilities and as life on the highest plane.

When we don't surrender, we lose precious treasure: abiding peace, love, faith, hope, power, abundance of life, rest for the soul. He ends with "life on the highest plane." What could be more valuable, more desirable, more prized than this?

It is similar to what Jesus described in his parable of the treasure hidden in a field. Jesus said, "The kingdom of heaven is like treasure hidden in a field, which someone found and hid; then in his joy he goes and sells all that he has and buys that field" (Matthew 13:44). Imagine that happening to you. You discover a treasure of immeasurable value in a field. To get the treasure you have to buy the field, which requires you to sell all that you have. Would you do so with regret? Of course not. You would sell all you have and experience joy.

Grace Adolphsen Brame puts it well: "This yes is an inner assent of the will. It is a willingness to receive the grace and the guidance of God. It can be so deep and far-reaching as to cause a real conversion of life, a real repentance, a turning around to go in a completely new direction." The true meaning of repentance is to change your mind, then change your way. Jesus often preached, "Repent, for the kingdom of heaven has come near" (Matthew 4:17). Change your mind, he is saying, about the kingdom. It is here. It is in your midst. You can enter it now. Taking this road will make all the difference.

Put simply, the yes of surrender is greater than the no of self-denial. What is gained is far greater than what is lost.

Put simply, the yes of surrender is greater than the no of self-denial. What is gained is far greater than what is lost.

PRAYING FOR SURRENDER

John Wesley (1703–1791) was the founder of Methodism. He was a man known for his deep piety. The Methodist movement in England and in the United States was one of the great movements in the history of the church. But Wesley was also an imperfect man, having many failures in his early ministry career. I find it encouraging to discover that our heroes of the faith were human. We fail, but we also get it right. One of the times Wesley was at his best was in his composition of a prayer, later called the Covenant Prayer (1775), which follows:

I am no longer my own, but thine.
Put me to what thou wilt, rank me with whom thou wilt.
Put me to doing, put me to suffering.
Let me be employed for thee or laid aside for thee,
exalted for thee or brought low for thee.
Let me be full, let me be empty.
Let me have all things, let me have nothing.
I freely and heartily yield all things to thy pleasure and disposal.
And now, O glorious and blessed God, Father, Son and
Holy Spirit,
thou art mine, and I am thine.
So be it.
And the covenant which I have made on earth,
let it be ratified in heaven.
Amen.

This is a prayer of utter surrender. It demonstrates great trust. In it Wesley is saying, "I will accept what you give me, *no matter what.*" This kind of prayer puts us in sync with the kingdom of God.

The second prayer of surrender that has been a blessing to me comes from St. Ignatius of Loyola (1491–1556). He was the founder of the Jesuits, a deeply committed and pious order within the Roman Catholic Church. Ignatius was going through a difficult time in his life, having suffered an injury to his leg in battle. He was feeling drawn to a life of complete commitment to God, but he had trouble leaving the comfortable life of a nobleman. He went on a retreat in Montserrat, and there Ignatius began to live his faith. He once spent an entire night in prayer before the statue of the Virgin. He put on simple clothes and gave his expensive clothing to a beggar.

Soon after, he began a period of eleven years writing what became one of the greatest works of Christian spirituality, the *Spiritual Exercises*. He, like Wesley, also penned one of the finest prayers of surrender ever written. It is called the Suscipe Prayer (pronounced *soos-keep-eh*, from the Latin word for "receive"), found toward the end of his *Spiritual Exercises*. I love the simplicity that underlies this short but potent "surrender" to God:

> Take, O Lord, and receive my entire liberty, my memory, my understanding and my whole will. All that I am and all that I possess, Thou hast given me: I surrender it all to Thee to be disposed of according to Thy will. Give me only Thy love and Thy grace; with these I will be rich enough and will desire nothing more. Amen.

Here Ignatius asks God to receive three aspects of who he is: his memory, understanding, and will. Like Wesley, he acknowledges that all he has is a gift from God; it is not his own. He surrenders it "all to Thee" in trust. Ignatius asks only for these two things: God's love and God's peace. If he were to receive these in exchange for his surrender, he notes, he would be "rich enough" and would "desire nothing more."

THE IMPERFECT WAY

With this arrangement of *surrender for joy*, of *obedience for riches*, it must be noted that this is neither easy nor done with complete perfection. I am sure that Willard, Elliot, Wesley, and Ignatius had their times of doubt, failure, and withdrawal. Ignatius wrote much about spiritual desolation. Even the great Mother Teresa wrote that she experienced times of struggle, doubt, and darkness. While some find this discouraging, I find it to be encouraging. She is a real person, a human being. None of us are strong and obedient every moment of our lives.

That is why I like the metaphor of a journey. We are travelers. We do not reach absolute perfection. True, we are called to offer ourselves "as a living sacrifice" (Romans 12:1). The problem with *living* sacrifices is that we sometimes want nothing more than to crawl off the altar. And we do.

The problem with living *sacrifices is that we sometimes want nothing more than to crawl off the altar.*

In "Hold Me, Jesus," the late singer and songwriter Rich Mullins sang,

Surrender don't come natural to me
I'd rather fight you for something
I don't really want
than to take what you give that I need

And we struggle and fight and learn and try again. We are here working with reality. The cost of nondiscipleship will never go away.

It will take us a while to live as Jesus' disciples, but when we do, a magnificent journey awaits us.

In the chapters that follow we will discover the way of surrender allows us

- to grow in the grace and knowledge of God
- to live our lives from above
- to listen to God
- to walk in faith
- to live with hope
- to demonstrate love
- to experience joy

The magnificent journey will lead us to the way of life we have been designed to live, a life deep in the kingdom of God.

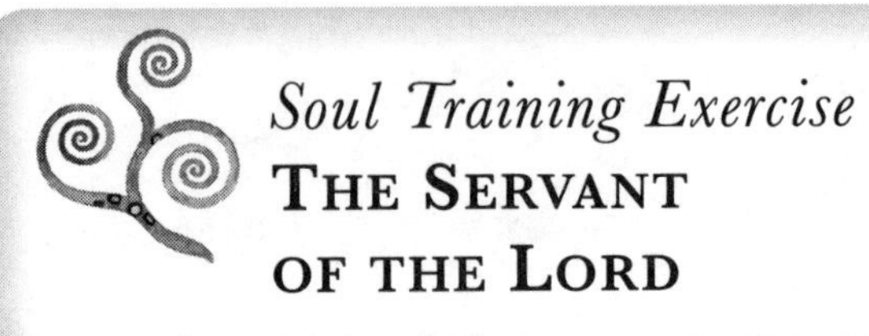

Soul Training Exercise
THE SERVANT OF THE LORD

I began to read the Holy Scriptures upon my knees, laying aside all other books, and praying over, if possible, every line and word. This proved meat indeed, and drink indeed, to my soul. I daily received fresh life, light, and power from above.

GEORGE WHITEFIELD

AT THE END OF EACH CHAPTER I invite you to try to practice Scripture meditation. The practice is simple. Read a passage from the Gospels slowly, trying to see it unfold in your mind. As you read the selected passage, try to *see* what is happening in your imagination. Try to imagine the people, the places, the sights, the smells, and the sounds. Place yourself as a bystander in the story. In all but this chapter and the last, the focus is on Jesus. Notice what the people (and angel in the following passage) say and do. If you find something compelling in this practice, be sure to write it down in your journal.

> In the sixth month the angel Gabriel was sent by God to a town in Galilee called Nazareth, to a virgin engaged to a man whose name was Joseph, of the house of David. The virgin's

> name was Mary. And he came to her and said, "Greetings, favored one! The Lord is with you." But she was much perplexed by his words and pondered what sort of greeting this might be. The angel said to her, "Do not be afraid, Mary, for you have found favor with God. And now, you will conceive in your womb and bear a son, and you will name him Jesus. He will be great, and will be called the Son of the Most High, and the Lord God will give to him the throne of his ancestor David. He will reign over the house of Jacob forever, and of his kingdom there will be no end." Mary said to the angel, "How can this be, since I am a virgin?" The angel said to her, "The Holy Spirit will come upon you, and the power of the Most High will overshadow you; therefore the child to be born will be holy; he will be called Son of God. And now, your relative Elizabeth in her old age has also conceived a son; and this is the sixth month for her who was said to be barren. For nothing will be impossible with God." Then Mary said, "Here am I, the servant of the Lord; let it be with me according to your word." Then the angel departed from her. (Luke 1:26-38)

SURRENDER PRACTICES

At the end of each chapter you will find several ideas of practices to take up. This is not a to-do list. Allow the Lord to draw you to the practice that is right for you in this season of life.

- Meditate on Wesley's Covenant Prayer until it is your own.
- Meditate on Ignatius's Suscipe Prayer until it is your own.
- Meditate on Tanner's *The Annunciation* painting until you can say, "Let it be."

2

Growing in Grace and Knowledge

Grow in the grace and knowledge of our Lord and Savior Jesus Christ. To him be the glory both now and to the day of eternity. Amen.

2 Peter 3:18

My daughter Hope was born in the year 2000. From the time she was in the womb till she was born and every day since, I have prayed for her. My prayer was that she would come to know Jesus and to live a vibrant Christian life. I did not merely want her to be a churchgoer. I had experienced a rich, interactive life with Jesus beginning in 1980. Her mother, my wife, Meghan, and I live Christ-focused lives. Hope was baptized as an infant (we are United Methodists) and spent her childhood Sundays in church. From the nursery to Sunday school to youth group, Hope was active in the life of the church. Still I prayed for a day that her faith would become *her* faith, not her parents' or her pastor's or her church's faith.

That day came the summer of her fourteenth year. She went to church camp and made fast friends with some strong believers. Hope had been through some difficult times, and she found in these friends grace, understanding, compassion, and support. They would become her "camp family." During the camp, a speaker encouraged the campers to trust Jesus. If they were facing something daunting, she told them to reach out to Jesus and let him be a part of their fear. The next day the campers got to go on a zipline. Harnessed to a suspended wire, a camper slides downward from thirty feet off the ground. As Hope waited her turn, she began to feel afraid. Then she remembered what the speaker had said: "Put your trust in Jesus."

So she did. With her knees knocking on the platform, she asked Jesus to give her courage. She immediately felt peace come over her. She leaped off the platform and glided down the zipline full of joy. As she unbuckled herself and walked away, she said to herself, *I really believe in Jesus*. When she got home she was eager to tell Meghan and me about her experience. We were overjoyed. Later I began to reflect on her story, and I must admit that a part of me thought it was kind of amusing. Jesus had used a zipline to enter her heart in a new way. A zipline!

Then I remembered C. S. Lewis's story of his conversion. He and his brother decided to go to the zoo, and Lewis rode in the sidecar of his brother's motorcycle. He said, "When we set out I did not believe that Jesus is the Son of God, and when we reached the zoo I did." Lewis, unlike Hope, was not scared of riding in the sidecar (though I would be!). He had been on a long journey toward faith. As an atheist, he could not arrive at a place of faith. However, he had become open to God, and God was waiting for the right moment, I believe. Somehow, miraculously, between the time he got in and got out of the sidecar, he became a believer. Apparently Jesus is fine with using sidecars and ziplines for these profound moments.

After this experience, Hope was eager to be a part of her church—youth group, Sunday school, small groups, worship—in a new way. I could tell she was not simply attending these gatherings, she was devouring them. She began reading the Bible regularly, listening to Christian music, attending Christian music concerts, and going on mission trips. Her commitment to Jesus influenced her entire life. She could not keep quiet around her friends at school. A girl at her school grew tired of her talking about Jesus and said disdainfully, "What are you now, some kind of Jesus freak?" Hope shot back quickly, "Yes, I am. I am a Jesus freak." She was very proud to be standing up for her faith, and we were proud of her.

Do you believe mystical experiences happen? Why or why not?

WHAT HAPPENED?

Skeptics might hear this story and think, *Well, that did not really happen. She was likely feeling some social pressure or a desire to imitate what the others said they were experiencing. Or maybe her brain just played a trick on her. Or maybe it was a surge of adrenalin that she interpreted as a religious experience.* Perhaps they would be correct. But in my experience this is *exactly* how the magnificent journey works. God is so big that he has to hide from us. If God appeared to us as he is, it would overwhelm us. But God wants to be seen and known, so the arrangement God has for us is this: If you seek me, you will find me.

Hope was seeking God. She was actually learning how to interact with the unseen but very real spiritual realm. To put it simply, she had a mystical experience. Some people find the word *mystical* to be some kind of magical or New Age word. *Mystical* means there was an element of mystery, something she could not fully describe, something for which words could not do justice. Hope turned to Jesus and expected Jesus to act. That is the essence of the magnificent journey of living as a Christ-follower: turn to Jesus and expect Jesus to act. When we turn to someone for something we cannot achieve on our own, we come with an admission of need. We come helpless. We come powerless. This is precisely the arrangement God has designed us for: learning to act in reliance on God.

> *Turn to Jesus and expect Jesus to act. That is the essence of the magnificent journey.*

This has been the arrangement from the beginning. Jesus has been making himself known and felt, through the Spirit, from the moment he rose from the grave. This is as he foretold:

> I have said these things to you while I am still with you. But the Advocate, the Holy Spirit, whom the Father will send in my name, will teach you everything, and remind you of all that I have said to you. Peace I leave with you; my peace I give to you. I do not give to you as the world gives. Do not let your hearts be troubled, and do not let them be afraid. (John 14:25-27)

The book of Acts depicts the early followers interacting with the spiritual realm, at times clumsily, at times heroically, but always learning to trust in it.

I suspect you, the reader, could tell stories similar to Hope's. From the moment I felt Jesus enter my life in August 1980, I have been experiencing God's action in my life. I rely on it. Were I to try to preach or teach or write in my own limited strength or smarts or cleverness, I would be failing those who listen to or read my words. I rely on God's *grace*, and it leads to *knowledge*, and that knowledge makes *faith* possible. Those are important terms that need clear definitions. I have learned that if we define our terms incorrectly, we will end up telling the wrong story.

GRACE, KNOWLEDGE, AND FAITH

Let me begin with what I have come to believe are *incorrect* definitions of these three terms that are common for many Christians. *Grace* is often defined as "unmerited forgiveness." *Knowledge* is limited to knowing the correct doctrine. And *faith* is thought of as "trying to believe what you really don't, which will somehow make God happy." I defined these terms this way as a young Christian, and I can attest that it ended up telling me the wrong story, which in turn led to living in frustration and fear. Thankfully, I have come to see that there is much more to these three powerful terms.

Grace is best defined as "God's action in our lives." Quite often we limit grace to "the forgiveness of sins." And while it includes forgiveness (it is one of God's most important actions), it is more than that. *Grace* means "gift" (Greek *charis*). It is unearned. We do nothing to deserve it. And it is incongruous. Into the world of sin and death comes God's saving act. We rebel from God, yet God dies for us. God's grace works paradoxically. God's grace is made powerful in our weakness (2 Corinthians 12:9). God is always acting for our good, even though it is unmerited.

I need God's grace for every aspect of my life. The air I breathe is an act of grace. The food I eat is an act of grace (which is why we say "grace" before meals). God nudges us, convicts us, comforts us, forgives us, restores us, reconciles us, and redeems us. In the magnificent story, God is the subject of many active verbs. God *loves*, God *heals*, God *dies*, God *rises*, God *descends*, and God *ascends*—all for our benefit. Each of these acts of grace are beautiful, good, and true.

Notice that when God acts, it is always *relational*. God does not act in isolation but always in relation. Therefore, these acts are known and felt in our experiences. This leads to knowledge, the second key word. *Knowledge* is the ability to represent something in an appropriate manner. When we know something, we can talk about it. I know about the game of tennis. I have played it and taught it and coached it. I know about backhands and forehands and serves and lobs. This knowledge is something I can put on paper, but mostly I know it experientially and relationally and bodily.

Grace is God's action in our lives.

When God acts for us relationally (grace) it leads to knowledge. That is why Peter can exhort us to "grow in . . . grace and knowledge" (2 Peter 3:18). If grace were limited only to forgiveness of sins, we could not grow in it (though we need it to grow). The more we create space for God to act in our life (what John Wesley called *means* of grace, such as prayer, fasting, and worship), the more we grow in knowledge. Once we obtain knowledge of something we can begin to act on that knowledge. That is faith.

Faith is the extension of knowledge based on knowledge. Because I know something (for example, that God is good and reliable), I can then act on it. Abraham is called the father of faith, most notably because he was willing to sacrifice Isaac. That appears to be a monstrous thing to do, but the key to the story is that Abraham had experienced God (grace) and had come to know God (knowledge) so that when God called on him to do something astounding, he did so by faith. Of course, we know that God stepped in and provided a ram for the sacrifice, once again teaching Abraham that he was not like the other gods.

A great example of grace, knowledge, and faith is the practice of *lectio divina*, particularly when it is done in a group. A group of people, expecting God to give them a word, listen for a word or phrase to stand out as a passage of Scripture is read. After a few readings, the people jot down the word or phrase that stood out. Next, they are asked to reflect and pray, asking God to help them understand. Then they write down what God is speaking to them. I have found that nearly every person has a word or phrase and can usually arrive at a conclusion about what God is saying. Most astonishing is when two people get the same word or phrase, and yet it means something different for them. Wow! The Spirit knows us so intimately! Finally, the participants are asked to find ways to act on the word they have been given, if that is appropriate.

The highlighting of the word or phrase by the Spirit is an act of *grace*. It then leads to a deeper *knowledge* of something we need to know. Finally, the Spirit may lead the person to act on that word or challenge, which is an act of *faith*. The more we engage in practices like *lectio divina* (including prayer, solitude, worship, etc.), the more we experience God's grace, the more we gain knowledge, and the more we can act in faith. We learn this important truth: we are not alone.

> *When God acts, it is always relational.*

WHAT IS ETERNAL LIFE?

In my journey a few Bible verses have restructured my understanding of the Christian life. John 17:3 is one of them: "This is eternal life, that they may know you, the only true God, and Jesus Christ whom you have sent."

I had spent all of my Christian life believing eternal life was something that would only happen after I died. Then I ran across this verse. It states clearly, "This is eternal life." But it says nothing about the afterlife or about having to die to experience it. It is simple and clear: eternal life is knowing God and Jesus Christ. In other words, eternal life is found in knowing two members of the Trinity: Father and Son. The Bible also tells us that we can only know the Father and the Son through the Spirit. So eternal life is found in knowing the Trinity.

In the Bible, knowledge almost never refers to what we call *head knowledge*. Knowledge does not refer to knowing facts about something or someone. Knowledge always refers to interactive relationship. In Amos 3:2, God tells the Israelites, "You only have I *known* of all the families of the earth" (emphasis added). Surely God *knew* about other nations. But Israel was the only nation God had interacted with, from Abraham and his children on. That is what the covenant was about: God wanted an interactive relationship with Israel. God was saying to them, "You are the only ones I have entered into covenant with."

The same is true of Mary. When she is told by Gabriel that she will bear a son, her response is "How shall this be, seeing I know not a man?" (Luke 1:34 KJV). Mary, of course, knew men. She had knowledge of men. But she did not have an interactive (in this case sexual) relationship with any man. So when Jesus says in John 17:3 that eternal life is *knowing* God and himself, he is talking about having an interactive relationship with them. When our life is caught up in God's life, our life becomes *eternal* life because it is a part of God's life.

Have you believed that eternal life happens only when you die? Do you now see it as a quality of life you can experience now?

God desires to know and be known. So when Hope called out for help, Jesus was glad, through the Spirit, to fill her heart with peace. This was something Hope *knew* not conceptually but experientially, not by exposition but by experience. Hope had experienced eternal life.

But what happens if we understand grace to be God's action in our lives? We then live each day, each moment, in expectation that God will act. We open the possibility that every aspect of our life—from gardening to parenting to our vocation—is an opportunity for God to interact with us. In fact, we can learn to count on it. We begin to see that we are not alone. God is with us, acting with us, accompanying us. This naturally leads to gratitude. We then thank God for his grace, his gift, his unearned interaction in our everyday lives.

And we will come to *know* God. When we embark on this magnificent journey, we *grow in the grace and knowledge of our Lord Jesus Christ*. This is the best invitation the world has ever been given. We learn to live the *with-God* life, which is none other than living in the kingdom of God. Jesus did not bring the kingdom of God into existence. The kingdom of God is from everlasting to everlasting. But Jesus freed the kingdom of God from its cultural, ethnic, and gender encrustation. Jesus' gospel, his proclamation of good news, was simply this: You can enter this way of living now, regardless of your ethnicity, gender, or sinful past. People have been taking him up on this offer ever since. Whenever people begin growing in the grace and knowledge of Jesus, the world becomes brighter.

SAUL, AUGUSTINE, AND SCIENCE MIKE

In the first century, a man named Saul was persecuting the members of a sect called the Nazarenes who were followers of Jesus. He was knocked off of his donkey by Jesus while on one of his persecution excursions. Jesus spoke to him. He told him to stop persecuting his people. He also told Saul he would be Jesus' messenger to the Gentiles—a mission he could never imagine taking. He was blinded and sent to a man named Ananias who healed his blindness. Saul, who became Paul, spent the next few years coming to know Jesus. Knowing Jesus—eternal life—was all Paul wanted. He said,

"I decided to *know* nothing among you except Jesus Christ, and him crucified" (1 Corinthians 2:2, emphasis added).

In the fourth century, a man named Aurelius Augustine wrestled with inner demons, mainly lust, until he began searching for a way out. He was a philosopher, a teacher or rhetor, and a scholar. Christianity seemed silly. But he was at the end of his rope. One day, while in Milan, he was with his friend Alypius and was weeping. Suddenly he heard the sound of children's voices, chanting, in Latin, *Tolle lege*, which means "Take and read." He went outside, but there were no children to be found. He saw a book of Paul's epistles sitting on a bench. Heeding the call to take and read, he opened the book, which fell to Romans 13. His eyes fell on these words: "Let us live honorably as in the day, not in reveling and drunkenness, not in debauchery and licentiousness, not in quarreling and jealousy. Instead, put on the Lord Jesus Christ, and make no provision for the flesh, to gratify its desires" (vv. 13-14). He wrote, "No further would I read; nor needed it: for instantly at the end of this sentence, by a light as it were of serenity infused into my heart, all the darkness of doubt vanished away." We call him St. Augustine today. He would go on to grow in the grace and knowledge of Jesus Christ.

In the twenty-first century a man named Mike McHargue also heard a voice. Raised a devout Southern Baptist, Mike had a crisis of faith. As a scientist, he found much of the Bible difficult to believe. He read many books by atheists and eventually became one himself—all while continuing to teach Sunday school at his church. But his soul was not at rest. He was still searching for answers. In his excellent book *Finding God in the Waves*, he tells about attending an invitation-only seminar. Mike shared his doubts with the group, and they did not reject him. They thanked him for his honest, searching questions.

The event ended with the group having communion together. At first Mike wanted to leave. He felt uneasy taking communion as a nonbeliever. He describes what happened next:

> The problem was that I couldn't take the bread without taking the metaphor. And that felt dishonest. I didn't believe that the body of Christ was broken for me, because I didn't believe that there was a body to break.
>
> I decided to walk away. But just when I was about to turn, I heard a voice say, "I was here when you were eight, and I'm here now."
>
> I froze, startled and amazed. I thought about hiding from bullies and talking to Jesus. . . .
>
> I thought about my best friend, a Jewish rabbi whom I'd never met in person but talked to more than anyone else. So I reached out, took the bread from Rob's hand. Then Rob said, "This is the blood of Christ, shed for you." I dipped the bread into the wine, and I ate it. I took the bread and the metaphor, and I ran from the room, my face full of tears. This is the part where I should explain the science of how a sane person can hear an audible voice in a room when no one has spoken. Believe me, I've spent a long time researching it, and I would love to explain it. I can't.

If that was all that happened that night, it would be enough. But the night was not over.

He walked out of the retreat house onto the beach and looked at the moon. He found himself praying for the first time in years. His prayers were mostly questions to God, but he ended by saying this: "All I know is, I met Jesus tonight." Then something happened. He writes,

> When I said the word *Jesus*, the waves rushed toward me. I was standing high up on the beach, 25 feet or more above the

waves, but the water still rushed up and over my feet—all the way up to my shins.

I thought about what Rob had said: that Christ's last act of service before His crucifixion was to wash the feet of His followers.

I said, "Is that you, God? Is this really happening?"

And the whole world fell away, like the veil lifted from the face of a bride on her wedding day.

Mike, known to many as "Science Mike," had an interactive experience with Jesus. And it was spectacular. He had experienced eternal life.

For you, is Christianity primarily rational or relational—or both?

WHAT IS AT STAKE?

The stories of Hope, C. S. Lewis, Augustine, and Science Mike are important—maybe now more than ever. We are coming out of an era (modernity) that put a heavy emphasis on the rational side of faith. Baby boomers are the last generation to have framed Christianity as a set of doctrines to believe, with little emphasis on the experiential, even mystical, aspect of life with God. Arguments for the authority (even the inerrancy) of the Bible became central, certainly to evangelical Christians. The same is true of the literal six-day creation. These and other black-and-white positions determined who was and was not a true believer. But we are in a new era in which the Bible is seen as God's Spirit-inspired, authoritative Word, but not as a science textbook. It is a work of art that has the power to transform lives.

Science Mike's story is profound. His crisis of faith resulted when those sacred doctrines began to crumble. Could he still believe in Jesus and believe in the theory of evolution? He assumed he could not. That was what he had been told. Faith is rational, not experiential, he assumed. But then something happened during communion and later standing on a beach. It was a mystical experience—*mystical* means it is a mysterious yet very real encounter. He could no longer argue. Jesus was real. That was true knowledge: relational and experiential. He now *knew* that Jesus was real, not based on an argument but on an experience.

No one argues with an experience. I have often said that when someone gives a *testimony* in a church service, it is often more profound and inspiring than the sermon. Why? Because no one says, "Well, that did not happen to her—God did not speak to [or heal, or awaken, etc.] her." A sermon is a series of conjectures, and no matter how insightful it is, I will take a testimony any day. What is at stake here is that the world is waiting to see if Christ-followers can attest to real, genuine—dare I say, mystical—experiences. Like Hope or Lewis or Augustine or Mike, they possess a kind of knowledge—an experiential, relational knowledge—that is *eternal life*. It is the kind of knowledge we all seek and the only kind of knowledge our postmodern world will trust.

This does not mean that our faith is not rational; nor does it mean that we cannot know and connect to God through truth. For example, saying the Apostles' Creed is an important practice for me. It connects me with truth. One clause of the Creed says, "He [Jesus] was conceived by the virgin Mary." While I believe it is true, I also want to connect with the spiritual reality of living in a world where that actually happens.

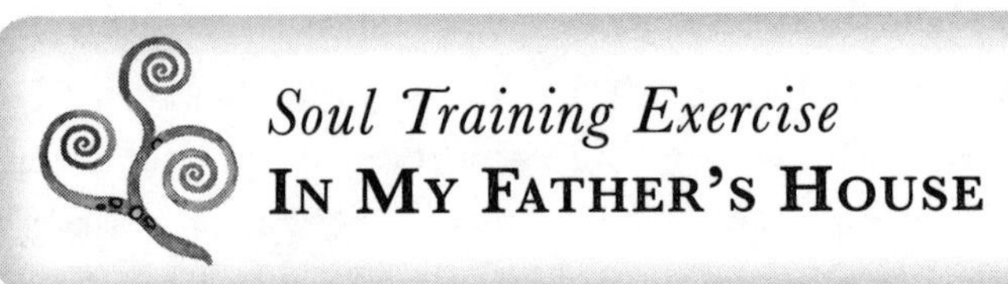

Soul Training Exercise
In My Father's House

I am a Jew, but I am enthralled by the luminous figure of the Nazarene. No one can read the Gospels without feeling the actual presence of Jesus. His personality pulsates in every word. No myth is filled with such life.

Albert Einstein

The practice is simple. Read a passage from the Gospels slowly, trying to see it unfold in your mind. As you read the selected passage, use your imagination to *see* what is happening. Try to imagine the people, the places, the sights, the smells, and the sounds. Place yourself as a bystander in the story. Put all of your focus on Jesus. Notice what he says and does. Allow his personality to pulsate in every word and action. If you find something compelling in this practice, be sure to write it in your journal.

I do not want to coerce you as you do this, or try to tell you what you should experience. Everyone's experience of the passage will likely be different. Ask the Spirit to help you see what you, uniquely, need to see.

CONTEMPLATING THE CHRIST FORM

> Every year his parents went to Jerusalem for the festival of the Passover. And when he was twelve years old, they went up as usual for the festival. When the festival was ended and they started to return, the boy Jesus stayed behind in Jerusalem, but his parents did not know it. Assuming that he was in the group of travelers, they went a day's journey. Then they started to look for him among their relatives and friends. When they did not find him, they returned to Jerusalem to search for him. After three days they found him in the temple, sitting among the teachers, listening to them and asking them questions. And all who heard him were amazed at his understanding and his answers. When his parents saw him they were astonished; and his mother said to him, "Child, why have you treated us like this? Look, your father and I have been searching for you in great anxiety." He said to them, "Why were you searching for me? Did you not know that I must be in my Father's house?" But they did not understand what he said to them. Then he went down with them and came to Nazareth, and was obedient to them. His mother treasured all these things in her heart. (Luke 2:41-51)

GROWING IN GRACE EXERCISES

This exercise can and usually does create a mystical encounter. I suspect if you were open to God engaging you in this experience, you felt or heard or thought something new. You gained a bit of *knowledge*, and that interaction was a work of God's *grace*.

Hope's prayer. Another practice for this week is to try Hope's prayer. Remember what she did? She heard the message that when you encounter a fear, allow Jesus to work with and in you. Ask Jesus to be near. When you encounter anything this week that causes fear or anxiety, pause to pray, asking Jesus to be with you, to hold you, to fill you with peace.

Eye spy. This week keep an eye out for the goodness, beauty, and truth that God places all around us. Keep a journal so you can reflect on what you have seen later in the week.

3

Living from Above

To be born "from above," in New Testament language, means to be interactively joined with a dynamic, unseen system of divine reality in the midst of which all of humanity moves about—whether it knows it or not.

Dallas Willard

Not long ago, I spoke at a daylong retreat for pastors and their wives. Each person was asked to read *The Good and Beautiful God* prior to the retreat. The host told me a bit about the people coming to the event, and let me know that there was one couple who could not get past the second chapter of the book. In that chapter I write about the death of our daughter Madeline and the pain and grief that my wife and I felt. This couple, the host said, had lost their son to a rare disease a year earlier. Their son was only fifteen. The host simply said, "It will likely not come up. But just in case, I wanted to give you a heads-up." I thanked him for making me aware of this situation.

During a break about halfway through the retreat, a man came up to me and said, "Would you have a few minutes after the retreat is over to visit with my wife and me?" I said I would be happy to. I knew in my spirit that this was the couple who stopped reading the book. When the day ended, this couple and I found a quiet place to sit and chat. The husband said, "You probably don't hear this much, but I have to tell you, I really didn't like your book." We all laughed. "Not because it is not a good book, but because it hit too close to our hearts. What you described was exactly what we went through. Your anger, your pain, your grief. Things you said were things we said, almost verbatim."

He then shared the story of their son's death. The mother said, "You wrote about how you went from painting your daughter's nursery to planning for her funeral. That was like us. We went from planning his birthday party to planning his funeral. He would have been sixteen." She began to weep. "Can you help us?" the father asked.

I said, "I am sorry that we are members of this club, meaning, people who have buried a child. It is unnatural for a parent to bury a child. But it happens, and we are both members of that club. The only encouragement I can offer is this: As Christians we grieve, to be sure, but as Paul wrote, we grieve differently because we have hope (1 Thessalonians 4:13). And we also have the assurance that God can and will work all things together for good (Romans 8:28). That is not to say that all *things* are good, but that God can work through all things for good. I don't mean to sound glib, but in truth, those two assurances—the hope of reuniting and the belief that God can work something good—are the two things that carried our family through."

I went on to talk about the world we live in, that it is not *secular* but sacred, that God is not distant but very near, that this is indeed a God-bathed world. I then talked about the collateral beauty that my wife and I had seen through Madeline's death. We saw a deep kindness from our community, an outpouring of love and support. We experienced a deepening in our own faith and a greater sense of God's goodness. We felt the better angels of our nature emerge. We now spoke about life's tragedies with a sense of depth. Of course, I pointed out that none of this was what we desired. It was what came as a result of living with faith and hope and with a God who is closer to us than we are to ourselves.

They then shared some of the amazing things that had come from their son's death. Later, I shared about how I came to write the book *Room of Marvels*, which tells of a waking dream I had about traveling to heaven, and how the book has been a blessing to many. I shared a story about a woman who read that book and gave sixty copies to her family and friends a month before her passing. She knew something they didn't, that she was dying, and she wanted her loved ones to grieve with hope. Her son told me this story and invited me to the funeral. It is astonishing that even in her dying she was so concerned with their grief.

God is not distant but very near; this is indeed a God-bathed world.

I told them I would send them a copy of the book and asked them to pray about the right time to read it. I believe God brings us the right books when we are ready. We prayed together, hugged, and they thanked me for my time. I responded, "No, thank you for sharing your sacred story with me. I will be praying for you." And I did. During my two-hour car ride I prayed over and over for them. Why? Because we live in a world where God hears our prayers, even the ones too deep for words. Because I have learned how to live *from above*, and that has made all the difference.

LIFE FROM ABOVE

A famous and oft-quoted Bible verse, especially during the Jesus movement in the 1970s, is John 3:3: "Very truly, I tell you, no one can see the kingdom of God without being born from above."

The King James Version translates those last words as "born again." *Born again* became a popular way to describe what happens to a person who has been "saved." The actual word used is best translated as born "from above" (which most modern translations do). While the difference in translation is subtle and may not seem to make much of a difference, there is a great deal at stake. As a new Christian, I was happy to embrace the fact that I had been born again. I even had a t-shirt that read, "I've been born again. Have you?" It was a not-so-subtle method of evangelism. Here is what is important: I was taught to believe that I was born again *once*. And that once I had been born again, I was saved. End of story.

But I had not been told that when Jesus spoke about being "born from above" he was talking about a new way of life or, to be more specific, living from another realm. Jesus used the word *above* quite often. He used it to refer to the heavenly places from which power comes. It is also the place Jesus has come from: "He said to them, 'You are from below, I am from *above*; you are of this world, I am not of this world'" (John 8:23, emphasis added).

Jesus, as a member of the Trinity, has come to us from the heavenly realm, which he simply calls "above." Paul also spoke about setting our hearts and minds on things above as an essential practice for Christ-followers: "If you have been raised with Christ, seek the things that are above, where Christ is, seated at the right hand of God. Set your minds on things that are above, not on things that are on earth" (Colossians 3:1-2).

This dichotomy between above and below can easily be misunderstood, as if Paul is encouraging a kind of otherworldly religion or escape from this world or a kind of vague spirituality.

Both Jesus and Paul are talking about two coexistent planes of human life. Things *below*, or things of earth, refer to the kingdoms of this world, which Paul called "the power of darkness" (Colossians 1:13). The values and power structures of the kingdoms of this world are built on force and violence, power and lust, greed and evil desires. Things *above*, or things of heaven, refer to the kingdom of God's Son, which believers have already been transferred into (Ephesians 2:4-6). To seek and to set our minds on things above means "to give Christ allegiance which takes precedence over all earthly loyalties." What does it look like to live on the plane we call "above"?

Is the paradigm shift from "born again" to "born from above" challenging to you? What difference might it make in your life with God?

THE HEAVENS ARE NOT IN SHORT SUPPLY

Jesus and Paul were not the first to understand the nature of the spiritual realm. One of my favorite stories in the Bible is found in Exodus 16. The people of Israel have been freed from slavery in Egypt and are wandering in the desert. They have not found enough food to eat and begin grumbling to Moses. The Lord tells Moses that he will send them food—in the form of manna—each morning. But he tells them to gather only enough for each day and no more; if they gather more, it will spoil and be filled with worms. On the sixth day, the day before Sabbath, they are to gather double portions, which they do, only this time the manna does not spoil. God is teaching them about provision and trust. I love one last part of the story. One evening they look out to see the earth covered with quails (Exodus 16:13). God wanted them to know God could throw a feast if God wanted to.

Jesus was certainly demonstrating this as well. His first miracle was turning water into wine (apparently of high quality). He turned a sack lunch into a massive meal for five thousand people. He made a fig tree wither and made withered hands whole. He walked on water, cast out demons, gave sight to the blind, and raised people from the dead. The point of all of this is that the provisions of the spiritual realm are beyond what we can ask or imagine. Where did all this power and provision come from? Above—the plane where Christ is, where we are called to set our minds and hearts and most of all our allegiance.

BORN FROM ABOVE: SPIRITUAL SENSES AWAKENED

What else does it mean to be born from above? It is to be regenerated by a power beyond us. In our cocrucifixion and coresurrection, we have been regenerated by a power greater than us. In John Wesley's sermon *The New Birth*, he explains that those who have not been born from above have physical senses (sight, hearing, smell, etc.), but they cannot connect with the spiritual realm. He writes,

> While a man is in a mere natural state, before he is born of God, he has, in a spiritual sense, eyes and sees not; a thick impenetrable veil lies upon them; he has ears, but hears not; he is utterly deaf to what he is most of all concerned to hear. His other spiritual senses are all locked up: He is in the same condition as if he had them not. Hence he has no knowledge of God; no intercourse with him; he is not at all acquainted with him. He has no true knowledge of the things of God, either of spiritual or eternal things; therefore, though he is a living man, he is a dead Christian.

However, once a person is born from above, their *spiritual senses* are awakened. He explains,

> But as soon as he is born of God, there is a total change in all these particulars. The "eyes of his understanding are opened;" and "he sees the light of the glory of God," his glorious love, "in the face of Jesus Christ." His ears being opened, he is now capable of hearing the inward voice of God, saying, "Be of good cheer; thy sins are forgiven thee;" "go and sin no more." He "feels in his heart," to use the language of our Church, "the mighty working of the Spirit of God;" he feels, is inwardly sensible of, the graces which the Spirit of God works in his heart. He feels, he is conscious of, a "peace which passeth all understanding.

Once we have been born from above, we can see God's glory, hear God's word to us, feel God's presence, taste and see that the Lord is good, and smell the fragrances of God's glory. This is essential if we are to journey deep into the kingdom of God.

LIVING WITHOUT WORRY AND FEAR

The world around us is scary. I find it hard to watch the news. Terrorism, earthquakes, and unnatural disasters seem to abound. But then I hear Jesus say, "Therefore I tell you, do not worry about your life" (Matthew 6:25). It sounds insane and impossible. But the kingdom of God is unshaken (Hebrews 12:28). In God's kingdom we learn that all things can and will work together for good (Romans 8:28). That is why Jesus' admonition to seek first the kingdom of God is so essential. Nothing, no angels or demons or principalities, can sever us from God's love. Not even death.

But when we learn the secret of life from above, we learn that what Jesus said is true: we will not taste death (John 8:52). I love the story of the great missionary Amy Carmichael when she was at the bedside of a five-year-old girl. Lulla was very sick and dying. They sent for medical missionaries, but one arrived too late. Carmichael recounts:

> It was in that chilly hour between night and morning. A lantern burned dimly in the room where Lulla lay. There was nothing in that darkened room to account for what we saw. The child was in pain, struggling for breath, and turning to us for what we could not give her. I left her and went to a side room, and cried to our Father to take her quickly. I was not more than a minute away, but when I returned she was radiant. Her little lovely face was lighted with amazement and happiness. She was looking up and clapping her hands as delighted children do. When she saw me she stretched out her arms and flung them around my neck as though saying goodbye in a hurry to be gone. And she did the same with the others. And then again holding her arms to someone we could not see, she clapped her hands. Had only one of us seen this thing we might have doubted it, but all three saw it. There was no trace of pain in her face. She was never to taste pain again. We saw nothing in that dear child's face but unimaginable delight. We looked where she was looking almost thinking we would see what she saw. What must the fountain of joy be if the spray from the edge of the pool can be like that?

What was little Lulla seeing? How far away was what she saw? She, like Jesus and Stephen and Peter, saw the heavens opened, right in her midst. Nothing, not even death, can separate us from it. Until then, we get occasional sprays from the edge of the pool, and we know we are safe.

Living from above also makes us strong. Julian of Norwich wrote, "If a man or woman . . . could see God, as God is continually with man, he would be safe in soul and body, and come to no harm. And furthermore, he would have more consolation and strength than all this world can tell." What a beautiful way of describing living from above: God continually *with* us. Safety, peace, and strength are the natural outflow of looking not at what can be seen but what is unseen.

ARRANGING YOUR DAYS TO EXPERIENCE LIFE FROM ABOVE

M. Scott Peck was quoted as saying that of all the inventions of the twentieth century, the most important one is the twelve-step program. This recovery program was created by Christian men, but they knew that if the language remained Christian it would prevent some from seeking help. So they changed the wording to make it more generic. However, the power of the twelve-step program is nothing other than learning how to live from above, accessing a power greater than ourselves because any power addicts possess is too weak to restore their lives to sanity.

The first step is to admit they are powerless over the addictive agent (alcohol, drugs, sex). That agent has become a *power*, and it has become a greater power than the addict. The second step is to believe that there is a power greater than ourselves that actually can restore us to sanity. This is a step of hope. On our own we lack the power to change, to recover who we were intended to be. The third step is to make a decision (once and always) to turn our will and our lives over to the care of God. This is a decision to quit quitting and to start relying on the power of God, which is far greater than the power of our addictive agent.

The first three steps form a process of liberation and transformation. We are essentially saying, "Yes, I have a problem. Yes, I believe there is a solution. Yes, I will accept that help." This three-step dance is the same as living from above. "I can't, you can, please help." We rely on the resources of the kingdom of God, on the realm of the Spirit, and on the power of God, who is greater than any obstacle we face. *This process works not just for the addict.* It is for all of us all of the time. Perhaps our problems are not as dire as those of people with addictions; nonetheless, God desires to act in our lives—our ordinary lives. Here are a few examples:

God desires to act in our lives—our ordinary lives.

- You have a problem with a coworker. You could try to use your cleverness to solve the problem. Or you could live from above by praying about it, allowing God to help you, keeping your eyes open to resources, events, and ways to better communicate.
- You are struggling as a parent to find the right ways to help your child who is struggling in school. You could try to assert your authority and force the child to do better, using reward and punishment. Or you could live from above and bathe your child in prayer, focusing on the reality that Jesus cares deeply for your child and does not worry about the child as you do. Entrust the matter to God and let your child know that you love and support them, and trust that they will find their way.
- You are working on a creative project and you get stuck. Instead of pushing and fussing and fretting (living from below), you could offer this project to God, asking God for wisdom and insight, for increased creativity, and for peace and calm in the meantime.

I like to call this *mysticism in the mundane.* We may be tempted to think that the ordinary events of our lives are not of interest to God. That is not true.

One of the best ways to arrange our days in order to live from above is to begin each morning looking over that day's schedule. There might be meetings to attend, people to meet, and projects to work on. Take each of those calendar events to God. I like to imagine Jesus with me throughout the day. This helps me to be more aware of his presence and more attentive to his voice. This does not mean we will not face any problems or setbacks, but it helps us to create the habit of setting our minds and hearts on things above, where Christ is (Colossians 3:1-3).

When you think about how God has acted in your life, would you consider yourself perhaps more mystical than you realized? If so, how does that strike you?

THE GOSPEL FOR UNBLESSABLE CONDITIONS

Of all of the grief and loss and hurt we must live through, rejection and suffering are among the most challenging. The couple I spoke about at the beginning of this chapter have found themselves in a humanly unblessable condition: the loss of a child. In these moments we discover whether or not we have grasped Jesus' gospel. Jesus' invitation into the with-God life in his everpresent and unshakable kingdom can and will bring comfort to us in times of suffering. When the doctor delivers bad news, or a loved one says they no longer love us, or a boss explains we have been let go, that is precisely when the gospel can enfold us. Jesus drew the least, the lost, and the lowest because they knew that in him—in the kingdom he was offering them—they would be blessed.

The gospel is not merely about managing our *sin* problem, it is also about our *suffering* problem. And the good news is that we who follow Jesus have had our eyes opened wide and are living in and from another world. God is with us in our joy and our suffering. That is what the gospel of Jesus tells me. It tells me I can live without fear, that I can live with joy, and that I can trust that all the things that happen to me and mine are ultimately in the hands of a good and beautiful and true God, who can make all things work together for good.

The gospel is not merely about managing our sin *problem, it is also about our* suffering *problem.*

An old maxim says that "time heals all wounds." I disagree. Time helps us gain stability in our wounds, but the pain remains. Our dear Madeline has been gone from us for twenty years, and that pain still remains, as real as the day she died. God does not take this pain away. The words of the great theologian Dietrich Bonhoeffer have given me great comfort:

> Nothing can make up for the absence of someone whom we love, and it would be wrong to find a substitute; we simply must hold out and see it through. That sounds very hard at first, but at the same time it is a consolation, for the gap, as long as it remains unfilled, preserves the bond between us. It is nonsense to say that God fills the gap; God does not fill it, but on the contrary, God keeps it empty and so helps us to keep alive our former communion with each other, even at the cost of great pain.

God, who is above but very near, does not fill the gap, and in so doing, keeps our communion with Madeline alive. That is one beautiful way we are living from above. God is teaching us about provision and trust.

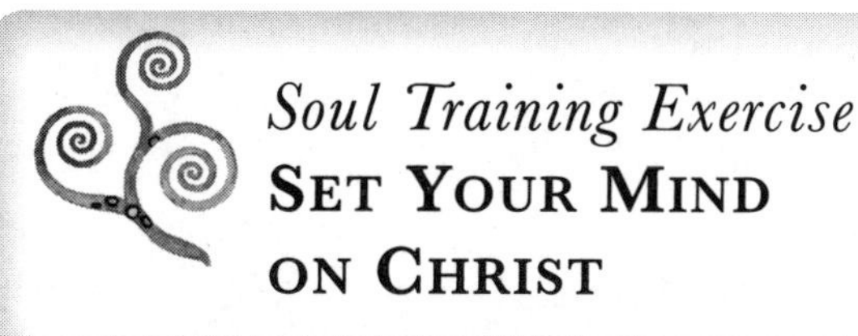

Soul Training Exercise
Set Your Mind on Christ

Let our chief endeavor be to meditate
on the life of Jesus Christ.

Thomas à Kempis

The practice is simple. Read a passage from the Gospels slowly, trying to see it unfold in your mind. As you read the selected passage, try to *see* what is happening in your imagination. Try to imagine the people, the places, the sights, the smells, and the sounds. Place yourself as a bystander in the story. Put all of your focus on Jesus. Notice what he says and does. Allow his personality to pulsate in every word and action. If you find something compelling in this practice, be sure to write it down in your journal.

CONTEMPLATING THE CHRIST FORM

> On the third day there was a wedding in Cana of Galilee, and the mother of Jesus was there. Jesus and his disciples had also been invited to the wedding. When the wine gave out, the mother of Jesus said to him, "They have no wine." And Jesus said to her, "Woman, what concern is that to you and to me?

> My hour has not yet come." His mother said to the servants, "Do whatever he tells you." Now standing there were six stone water jars for the Jewish rites of purification, each holding twenty or thirty gallons. Jesus said to them, "Fill the jars with water." And they filled them up to the brim. He said to them, "Now draw some out, and take it to the chief steward." So they took it. When the steward tasted the water that had become wine, and did not know where it came from (though the servants who had drawn the water knew), the steward called the bridegroom and said to him, "Everyone serves the good wine first, and then the inferior wine after the guests have become drunk. But you have kept the good wine until now." Jesus did this, the first of his signs, in Cana of Galilee, and revealed his glory; and his disciples believed in him. (John 2:1-11)

LIVING FROM ABOVE EXERCISE

This week try to set your mind and heart on the place "where Christ is, seated at the right hand of God" (Colossians 3:1). As you go about your days, be mindful of the nearness of this other plane of reality we call the kingdom of God, which is right in our midst. Remind yourself that your highest allegiance is not to the kingdoms of this world but rather to the kingdom of God's beloved Son.

4

Listening to God

Why is it that when we speak to God
we are said to be praying, but when God speaks
to us we are said to be schizophrenic?

Lily Tomlin

I was teaching a class called Introduction to Religion. We were reading William James's classic book *Varieties of Religious Experience*. In the book James discusses the many ways people encounter God. I asked if anyone in the class had ever had a religious experience, or if they ever felt addressed by God and would be comfortable sharing about it. The class went silent, with heads looking down at the desks (a classic "please don't call on me, professor" move).

"Okay, well, I have," I said. I began to share some of the times I felt God was speaking to me. After I finished there was silence. Then a hand went up. A young man shared a time when he was walking in the woods and he heard God speak to him. He did not want to share the content of what God said because it was personal.

I told him I understood and thanked him for sharing. A few moments of silence passed and then another hand went up, then another, then another. The entire class period was spent hearing people share stories of religious experiences and divine interaction. Nearly everyone shared a story, and I suspect they all would have if we had not run out of time.

At the end of the class I asked them if they had shared their stories with anyone else before. They all shook their head no. I asked why. One young woman said, "They are very personal. And it is hard to know if it was really God or just something we made up. Besides, most people would think you are crazy. It is better to keep it to yourself." And most people do. Unless a person feels safe in sharing these kinds of events, they do not share them. I suspect another reason people fail to share these stories is that it might make them seem special. "Wow, God spoke to you—you must be holy or something."

Tanya Marie Luhrmann is a psychological anthropologist and professor in the department of anthropology at Stanford University. Her research among evangelical Christians on the subject of hearing God led her to say this:

> For most of them, most of the time, God talks back in a quiet voice they hear inside their minds, or through images that come to mind during prayer. But many of them also reported sensory experiences of God. They say God touched their shoulder, or that he spoke up from the back seat and said, in a way they heard with their ears, that he loved them. Indeed, in 1999, Gallup reported that 23% of all Americans had heard a voice or seen a vision in response to prayer.

The number she cites is probably accurate. It is happening more than people feel comfortable admitting. To be sure, most Christians

I know feel comfortable saying that they were moved by something said in a sermon, as if God was speaking directly to them through the preacher. But few claim to have had God speak with them the way we see God speak to the people in the Bible.

Discerning God's voice is an essential part of eternal living, of living from above. Through learning to hear the words of God, we come to have the mind of Christ, which is essential if we are to live fully in the kingdom of God. To be born from above is to be made alive to the spiritual kingdom of God. One of the marks of the new birth is the ability to hear and apply God's word spoken to each of us individually. The gospel, as explained in *The Magnificent Story*, pulls us into this new world *now*, not when we die. We are now participants in the kingdom. This is also what it means to "grow in grace." The Bible is full of these kinds of stories and gives witness to God's desire to interact with us here and now.

Discerning God's voice is an essential part of eternal living, of living from above.

THE BIBLICAL WITNESS

The biblical witness about God speaking to humans is astounding. From Genesis ("Adam, where are you?") to Revelation ("The one who testifies to these things says, 'Surely I am coming soon.'"), God is constantly communicating with people. Jacob falls asleep and awakens to see something astonishing: "Jacob woke from his sleep and said, 'Surely the Lord is in this place—and I did not know it!' And he was afraid, and said, 'How awesome is this place! This is none other than the house of God, and this is the gate of heaven'" (Genesis 28:16-17). As we saw in the opening chapter, heaven is in our midst.

In 1 Samuel 3:1 we learn that the "the word of the LORD was rare in those days; visions were not widespread." That is, until Samuel heard his call in a mysterious way. The Lord called for Samuel in an audible voice, but thinking it was his master, Eli, Samuel went into Eli's room, only to have Eli say, "I did not call for you." This happened two more times, until Samuel finally realized it was God. The Lord said to Samuel, "See, I am about to do something in Israel that will make both ears of anyone who hears of it tingle" (1 Samuel 3:11).

Perhaps the most famous Old Testament story about the voice of God is in 1 Kings 19:11-12. Elijah was on the run in the wilderness and made his way into a cave. Suddenly there was a loud wind, then an earthquake, then a fire, but the Lord was not in any of these. Then suddenly there was a still, small voice (v. 12 KJV), and that is when Elijah heard the voice of God. The still, small voice of God seems to be God's preferred way to speak. I think this is because God does not want to overwhelm us with the spectacular but to soothe us in stillness.

> *Have you ever lamented how often we have the experience of Jacob, who said, "Surely the LORD is in this place—and I did not know it"?*

I love the story of Elisha and the King of Aram who was at war with Israel. The king kept passing on secret war tactics to his men, but Elisha was able to hear the king's words spoken in his bedchamber (talk about a surveillance device!). When the king of Aram discovered this, he sent his horses and chariots to seize Elisha. When Elisha's servant told him that he was surrounded, Elisha said,

> "Do not be afraid, for there are more with us than there are with them." Then Elisha prayed: "O LORD, please open his

> eyes that he may see." So the Lord opened the eyes of the servant, and he saw; the mountain was full of horses and chariots of fire all around Elisha. (2 Kings 6:16-17)

Chariots of fire appeared in the unseen realm. Elisha was in communication with angels. These kinds of experiences appear throughout the Bible. Are they telling something real, or are they myths?

The New Testament is equally full of these kinds of stories. At Jesus' baptism the heavens were opened and a voice was heard: "This is my beloved Son." Throughout the Gospels, Jesus is in constant communication with his heavenly Father. It is an ongoing interaction. In John 17, we see Jesus at prayer, speaking directly to God, praying that we would have eternal life (which is knowing the Father and Son [v. 3]) and that we would be one, as they are one (v. 11).

Jesus made it clear that his followers would recognize his voice. Comparing us to sheep with Jesus as our shepherd, he said, "The gatekeeper opens the gate for him, and the sheep hear his voice. He calls his own sheep by name and leads them out. When he has brought out all his own, he goes ahead of them, and the sheep follow him because they know his voice" (John 10:3-4). Finally, Jesus spoke directly to Paul:

> Now as he was going along and approaching Damascus, suddenly a light from heaven flashed around him. He fell to the ground and heard a voice saying to him, "Saul, Saul, why do you persecute me?" He asked, "Who are you, Lord?" The reply came, "I am Jesus, whom you are persecuting. But get up and enter the city, and you will be told what you are to do." (Acts 9:3-6)

One of the more amusing verses in the Bible, for me, is found in Acts, when the disciples are debating about whether or not the Gentiles must adhere to all of the Jewish practices. Presumably they were listening to the voice of the Spirit, for they concluded,

"It has seemed good to the Holy Spirit and to us to impose on you no further burden than these essentials" (Acts 15:28). I find it amusing to think they sat around and listened to the Spirit, who said something like, "Yeah, it seems good to me, fellas."

Skeptics can hear every one of these stories and say, "Well, these are just myths and make-believe. They are ancient stories full of wild claims to have heard from God and the angels. But they simply did not happen. There is absolutely no proof." And they are right that we have no proof. We have only the testimony of those who put pen to parchment and told us what they experienced. Such stories do not end with the Bible.

THROUGHOUT HISTORY

From the earliest Christians to Christ-followers of our day, men and women have given witness to countless experiences of hearing the voice of God and interacting with the heavenly realm. To name all of the significant figures in Christian history who have been addressed by God, and to tell their stories, would take up more ink and pages than I have room for in this book. Everyone with "Saint" in front of their name (from Patrick to Francis to Teresa) had many divine encounters. The great Reformers such as Luther, Calvin, and Wesley claimed to have heard from God in many different ways. In more modern times, figures like Martin Luther King Jr. testified to hearing directly from Jesus. In the winter of 1956, while sitting in fear at his kitchen table, terrified about what might happen to him and his family during the Montgomery bus boycott, Dr. King said he heard the voice of Jesus speak directly to him, "I will be with you." King said it gave him the courage to continue the movement.

The great hymns of our faith history attest to the presence and voice of God. From "Be Thou My Vision" ("Thou my best thought, by day or by night, waking or sleeping, thy presence my light") to

"Come, Thou Fount of Every Blessing" ("Jesus sought me when a stranger, wandering from the fold of God") to "He Leadeth Me" ("He leadeth me, O blessed thought! O words with heavenly comfort fraught") to "I Need Thee Every Hour" ("I need thee every hour, most gracious Lord; no tender voice like thine, can peace afford") to my favorite of all, "In the Garden":

> He speaks, and the sound of his voice
> Is so sweet the birds hush their singing,
> And the melody that he gave to me
> Within my heart is ringing:
> And he walks with me, and he talks with me,
> And he tells me I am his own,
> And the joy we share, as we tarry there,
> None other has ever known.

For centuries Christian women and men have sung these words to proclaim the glorious truth that God is not silent, that God is not distant but is present. God seeks us, God leads us, and his tender voice brings peace and joy.

IS IT REALLY GOD?

When I read these stories from the Bible, stories from the lives of Christ-followers through the ages, and the words of these hymns, I find them convincing and motivating. I want that kind of interaction with God. But there is one problem we must address: uncertainty. The first problem we encounter when it comes to hearing God is the difficulty of knowing if it is really God. I am more like Gideon, who after hearing a word from the Lord, responded by saying, "Show me a sign that it is you who speak with me" (Judges 6:17).

I have come to believe that God does not—for the most part—overwhelm us with a word that leaves no doubt. Moses got a burning bush and Paul got knocked off of his donkey, but by and large God speaks to us in ways that leave room for questions and doubt. If, while I was searching for an answer in prayer, God spelled out the answer in my alphabet soup, this would leave little room for doubt. I might be able to say, "What a coincidence. The words 'Marry Julie Jones' appeared in my soup today. That's weird. I wonder what I should do."

I think doubt and uncertainty are a part of God's communication with us. Doubts, said Frederick Buechner, are "ants in the pants of faith." They keep us moving. They prevent complacency. So if you have sensed God speaking to you through a sermon, a friend, a Bible verse, or a gentle voice and wondered *Was that God?*, that is perfectly normal, even to be expected. This uncertainty sets you on a journey to pursue whether or not it was in fact a word *for* you or *from* you.

Do you think we talk enough about doubting in the church? Why or why not?

MANY FORMS OF COMMUNICATION

Let's begin with a simple question: How does God speak to us? In the Bible we see God speaking directly to individuals. Sometimes it is through a burning bush, sometimes an angel, sometimes a still, small voice. The ancients did not have the Bible as we have it. But God spoke to them, and we have a written record of their interactions with God. The Bible is, after all, a written record of God speaking to God's people—of which we are now members. In the Bible we see God speaking through dreams, through prophecy, and through other people in the church: "When you come together, each one has a hymn, a lesson, a revelation, a tongue, or an interpretation. Let all things be done for building up" (1 Corinthians 14:26). In the Bible we see God speak through a voice, through a phenomenon, through a phenomenon plus a voice (the burning bush, Jesus' baptism), through visions, through human voices, through the still, small voice, and through angels.

God still speaks to us today in many ways. God speaks to me quite often through the words of other people, for example. God speaks to me when I become silent and open in a listening posture. God speaks to me through the example of other people.

God also speaks to us through sermons, conversations, literature, movies, and songs. I believe God employs all of these different ways of communicating so we do not depend on one single channel of communication. One of the most amazing phenomena I experience as a preacher is that after I give a sermon, people sometimes say to me, "Thank you. God really spoke to me through your sermon." Sometimes I ask what God spoke to them, and more often than not what they heard God saying to them was something I did not say. I know because I went back and read the notes and even listened to the sermon. I call this "God speaking between the lines."

For us today, the Bible is first and foremost God's preferred way of speaking to us. This can be a challenge to those who grew up with a view that the Bible is a book to read and study but not a book in which God speaks directly to individuals. I have had many students who grew up in churches where the Bible is seen as only a place to affirm doctrinal positions. They have been challenged, particularly in our class The Bible in Christian Spiritual Formation, to see that the Bible is a living, breathing word. The Bible is, to be sure, a reliable text for doctrinal foundation, but it is inspired by the Holy Spirit who still uses it to inspire us today.

THE IMPORTANCE OF MOTIVE

Many want to know God's will, or the future, as a means of gaining knowledge for power. The only right motive is to become more Christlike. In my experience, God becomes a lot more communicative when I am in this posture. When I begin my day saying, "Lord Jesus, I want to be more like you. I want your help. I need your help. My desire is to grow in my knowledge and image of you," I find God's communication to me becomes greater and stronger.

Why is this important? I confess to seeking God's voice or word or guidance sometimes as a means to power. It is not like I pray, "Lord, tell me if the Yankees are gonna win tomorrow so I can place a bet." It is more subtle: "Lord, tell me which way to do such and such," not to be more like Jesus but to increase my effectiveness or to improve my performance. When it comes to hearing God, motive matters. That is because prayer is not for receiving a magic word but for establishing a relationship with God that will lead to transformation. We cannot fool God. God always knows our motive, so it is best to be honest.

> *"When it comes to hearing God, motive matters." How does that resonate with you?*

I think Jesus loves it when we come to the Bible with the right motive. As I shared in the first chapter in the story of my trip to the monastery, I went with the wrong motive. I was in control of the Bible. I interpreted the Bible—it did not interpret me. It was only when I finally broke down and surrendered that I came to the Bible with the right motive. Then the Spirit was able to speak to me through the story of the Annunciation, which forever changed my life. All it took was a persistent jogging monk, a room without a view, and the wooing of the Holy Spirit.

THE NECESSARY SILENCE

God will not tell us what to do every moment of the day or for every decision we must make. If a parent stood over a child and told them what to do every moment of every day, the child would never grow and mature. Besides hindering development, it also leads to paranoia. We begin to doubt we can make the right decision on our own. "God, please tell me your perfect will every second of the day." That prayer will be met with silence.

More than once I have played Bible roulette, randomly opening the Bible and blindly putting my finger down on the page, hoping I will be given the secret answer. Come to think of it, that practice is more like the Ouija board than roulette. It is more superstition than prayer. It is more like magic than conversation. God wants relationship. Quite often we just want a word so we can bypass having to use our God-given minds.

However, I have a friend who was once in a very real, very dark place. She describes it as a time when she was reaping the consequences of her own sins. She felt distant from God. A friend gave her a Bible, and one night, all alone, at the end of her rope, she grabbed the Bible and randomly opened it and placed her hand on the page. Beneath her finger was Matthew 6:26: "Look at the birds of the air; they neither sow nor reap nor gather into barns, and yet your heavenly Father feeds them. Are you not of more value than they?" She wept for the next ten minutes, not out of sadness but out of joy. Even at her worst, even though she had not "shaped up," God was speaking to her: "I am with you." Her life began to turn around after that night. That was eighteen years ago. Even today she keeps a tiny bird statue on her mantle to remind her of what God spoke to her that night. I suspect it is not God's preferred manner, but if all we have is Bible roulette, God will likely use it.

I recognize that this may be a shift for those who have been taught that God's desire is to speak into every area of our lives, every single moment. Some assume that God wants to tell me what shirt to wear, what radio station to listen to, and what I should say to everyone I speak with. For example, I have a friend who prays for good parking places. He swears it makes a difference. I have never felt called to do that—mostly because I need the exercise, but also because I have come to believe that God would like me to work some things out on my own. And in the many places where I cannot do so, God is happy to provide me what I cannot do on my own.

TESTING THE WORD

The Bible is full of stories of *God speaking to people*. Some today assume that God stopped doing that after the books of the Bible were complete. Others struggle with whether they are *worthy* of having God speak to them. Still others may feel like they are novices with no real experience and no idea where to begin. If any of these describe where you are, then the first step is for you to ask for the faith to believe that God will speak to you (though perhaps not as clearly as he did to Abraham, Moses, Samuel, and David). Start small. Ask God to speak to you through a Bible passage or perhaps a sermon or a podcast. If you are feeling brave, ask God to speak to you through a gentle voice inside your head. A rule of thumb in spiritual formation is this: do what you can, not what you can't.

When you sense God has spoken to you in some way, it is good to *test* that word, especially if it is about something important, such as a major life decision. We must be aware of the possibility of the devil interfering with our hearing. I often pray for protection before engaging in communication with God. One surefire way of knowing if a word is not from God is in what it is calling you to do. If the word is calling you to love, forgive, bless, and serve, it is not from the devil. There are three common ways through which we can test these words: the Bible, circumstances, and other persons.

Any word from God must correspond with what is taught in the Bible. By that I mean it must be in line with the major tenets of Scripture. To be sure, the Bible does not have the answer about which job you should take, but it does contain basic principles that must not be violated. The major tenets of the Bible are things such as loving God and loving others in the manner you love yourself. Things like honesty, truth telling, humility, reverence for God, and self-sacrifice for the good of others are a part of the general teaching. You can be sure if you get a word that committing adultery is God's will, you heard wrong.

Circumstances often are a sign of confirmation. When I am praying and listening and I sense a word, situations often confirm—or deny—that word. And these situations can then be taken to a trusted friend for advice. For example, I had been seeking God's guidance on adding another member to the Apprentice Institute advisory board. I sensed the person who would be a great fit for this is Rebecca Willard Heatley, Dallas Willard's daughter. That same day I got an email from Rebecca. I sensed right away this circumstance was confirmation. But I was not sure, and this was a big decision, so I called a mutual friend, Jan Johnson, and asked her thoughts. She said, "Jim, that is strange. I have been thinking the same thing, but did not know you were adding someone. Yes, yes, this would be great." I am grateful that we have been given ways to affirm and confirm the guidance God gives us.

Circumstances often are a sign of confirmation.

VOICE RECOGNITION

The most common question I get from people is, What does God's voice sound like? My answer is, "A lot like mine." For me, God speaks in English. God speaks in a similar pattern, tone, and style as I do when I speak silently to myself. God speaks in thoughts, or more specifically, through *our* thoughts. This may seem to discredit the authenticity of his voice ("Jim, you are just talking to yourself and pretending it is God speaking"). But how gracious of God to make God's thoughts my thoughts. I count on God to show me the difference, and he does. It is a matter of learning how to listen and distinguish.

There are many factors in voice recognition. Just as with a human voice, we come to know a voice through its quality, tone, and style of speech. My friend Jane has a distinctive, lovely, soft North Carolina accent. I have heard her speak a lot, and I can close my eyes and hear her voice. When I pick up the phone and hear her say, "Hello, Jim," I know in an instant that it is Jane.

For me the voice of God, heard in my thoughts, has a specific quality and tone. The only words I can use to describe it are *gentle authority*. E. Stanley Jones writes, "The inner voice of God does not argue, does not try to convince you. It just speaks, and it is self-authenticating. It has the feel of the voice of God within it." God's words to me have always been peaceful. Not always comforting—I have been challenged by God as much as comforted—but never angry.

One day at a faculty meeting, I opened up my Mac laptop and hit the start button. It was during a moment of silence, so the familiar sound that a Mac makes when it starts was heard by those around me, causing me a moment of embarrassment. Sitting in front of me was one of our music professors, Cindy Blasdel. She turned to me and held up a notepad with these words on it: "F major triad in root position." I had no idea what this meant. Then I realized, her keen ears heard that sound and knew its musical composition. I later asked about how she knew this just by hearing it (by the way, neither she nor her husband or colleagues own a Mac).

She said, "Some people are born to know sounds, like that one, and others have to work hard to discern it. I teach a class called Oral Skills, and it is required for all music majors for four semesters. They learn how to analyze sounds. I play a note or sound, and they have to tell me what I played by either playing it back or singing it back or writing it down in musical terms."

She went on to say, "The F major triad in root position is a very settling, very positive sound. And it is complete. It is all-encompassing."

"Perhaps the people at Apple knew what they were doing when they chose that sound," I said, and continued, "I find this fascinating. What your students go through is similar to the process one undergoes when trying to discern the voice of God."

"Yes," Cindy said, "it is the same. In both cases, you have to choose to learn."

THE STILL, SMALL VOICE

I believe "the still, small voice"—or the interior, or inner voice—is God's preferred and most valuable form of personal communication. This is because it fits best with God's character; God wants to engage us without violating our freedom and growth. Burning bushes leave little room for doubt. The still, small voice is gentle and nonintrusive. It allows us to enter the dialogue freely.

Not long ago God spoke to me three times in one day. One involved selecting a person for a ministry event I was hosting. Another was deciding on a theme for another event down the road. The other involved a fundraising project. There was interconnection in all three of these words from God, which means the answers that came were confirmed by several other events and factors. In short, it made sense. However, someone might say one or two things about my experience.

One would be, "Well, Jim, you are a writer, a thinker, a creative type. You just came up with those solutions on your own." To that I would respond, "I am not that smart or creative. In each case, the word given came, as they say, 'out of the blue.' The answers had never occurred to me." The other response to my claim might be, "Wow, Jim, you are a saint!" To that I would respond, "Wrong. I am no saint. Ask my wife. I am just doing a yeoman's work. I have been walking and talking with Jesus for over thirty years. I have read the Bible through twice, spent one summer meditating on all of the psalms, spent a year in deep study of Wesley's sermons, spent time in solitude and prayer, and have been journaling from the beginning. I am no saint, but I have been showing up."

CREATING CONDITIONS

The first condition for hearing God is to show up. We cannot force God to speak to us. But we can create the conditions. The following are a few:

- Be willing to obey.
- Ask God to speak to you.
- Never limit how God can speak to you. Here is a good prayer: "God, speak to me today. I will be listening. Speak through people, through circumstances, through a book, or through nature. If you want to use a burning bush, I am ready. If you want to speak in a still, small voice, I am ready. I am all ears today."
- Create space through silence.

William Penn said, "The more silent, the more suitable to the language of the Spirit." Dallas Willard said, "Generally it is much more important to cultivate the *quiet, inward space of a constant listening* than to always be approaching God for specific direction."

> *We cannot force God to speak to us. But we can create the conditions.*

WHAT IS AT STAKE?

After reading this chapter, you may feel inspired to become "all ears for God." Or you may remain skeptical. But consider this: What if you never engaged in hearing God? The result would be missing out on the following:

- an all-access pass to the kingdom of God
- guidance and direction for the things you need
- discernment for difficult decisions
- character that comes as a result of obedience to the words given
- faith, hope, and love

In 1 Corinthians 13, Paul speaks of a day when prophecies and tongues and words of knowledge will end (v. 8). But there are three things that will never end: faith, hope, and love (v. 13). Those are the subjects of chapters five through seven.

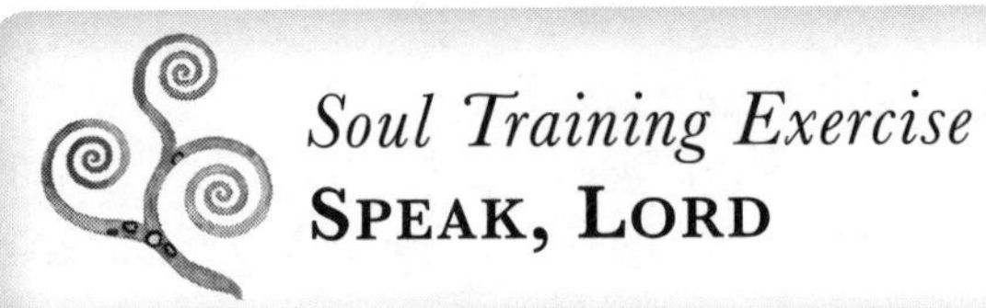

Soul Training Exercise
SPEAK, LORD

We live, in fact, in a world starved for solitude, silence, and private: and therefore starved for meditation and true friendship.

C. S. LEWIS

THE PRACTICE WE HAVE BEEN DOING after each chapter is simple. Read a passage from the gospels slowly, trying to see it unfold in your mind. As you read the selected passage, try to *see* what is happening in your imagination. Try to imagine the people, the places, the sights, the smells, and the sounds. Place yourself as a bystander in the story. Put all of your focus on Jesus. Notice what he says and does. Allow his personality to pulsate in every word and action. If you find something compelling in this practice, be sure to write it down in your journal.

CONTEMPLATING THE CHRIST FORM

> So again Jesus said to them, "Very truly, I tell you, I am the gate for the sheep. All who came before me are thieves and bandits; but the sheep did not listen to them. I am the gate. Whoever enters by me will be saved, and will come in and go

out and find pasture. The thief comes only to steal and kill and destroy. I came that they may have life, and have it abundantly.

"I am the good shepherd. The good shepherd lays down his life for the sheep. The hired hand, who is not the shepherd and does not own the sheep, sees the wolf coming and leaves the sheep and runs away—and the wolf snatches them and scatters them. The hired hand runs away because a hired hand does not care for the sheep. I am the good shepherd. I know my own and my own know me, just as the Father knows me and I know the Father. And I lay down my life for the sheep. I have other sheep that do not belong to this fold. I must bring them also, and they will listen to my voice. So there will be one flock, one shepherd. For this reason the Father loves me, because I lay down my life in order to take it up again. No one takes it from me, but I lay it down of my own accord. I have power to lay it down, and I have power to take it up again. I have received this command from my Father." (John 10:7-18)

HEARING PRACTICE

This week make Samuel's prayer your own. He said, "Speak, Lord, for your servant is listening" (1 Samuel 3:9). Take a few deep breaths in a few moments of silence and pray this prayer. Try to be still and listen. Keep a journal nearby to record any word you receive.

Part Two

DEVELOPING KINGDOM VIRTUES

5

Relaxing into Faith

Great faith, like great strength in general,
is revealed by the ease of its workings. . . . Most of what
we think we see as the struggle of faith is really the struggle
to act as if we had faith when in fact we do not.

Dallas Willard

Steve has been a friend, a mentor, and an example for me in the area of business and leadership. Steve is a very successful CEO of a large company. He is a dedicated Christ-follower, and his faith influences every area of his life. But it was not always that way. After college Steve had a number of jobs in which he worked hard and worked his way up in business. Eventually he was hired by a large company and was successful in that job. His faith life, however, was separated from his work and his family life. Steve likes to say he had all of these areas of his life in separate boxes. God, work, family, health, finances—each aspect of his life was in its own box. Steve said, "Faith was not a part of every area of my life. What I missed was that in my work life I thought outcomes were *my* responsibility. As a result I held on too tight; I was the one in control. That becomes very difficult to handle when you do all the right things, kingdom things, and the outcome is negative. The consequence of this is that work was 'my kingdom.'"

Then something happened that would lead to a major change. A coworker who was on Steve's level was going to stage a coup to get their superior ousted. He wanted Steve and two other coworkers to go in on it with him. As people of character, Steve and these two others refused. After the coup happened, and when this coworker gained power, he got Steve fired. Suddenly Steve was without a job. He had saved well and knew he had enough money to survive for a year or so. What happened next would not only turn around his career but would also save his soul—and be of great help to the many people who would one day work for him.

Steve said, "I saw my work as *mine*. Work was what *I* did. God was not a part of my work life at all. But after I got fired I reevaluated my life. I felt God calling me to surrender, in humility, and to rip open the boxes, and to integrate God in every area of my life—especially my work life. I knew this in my head, but my heart was not ready for it. I spent seven long and painful months trying to make this change. I finally did. I remember the exact moment the change occurred—I was driving on the highway, at the intersection of K-96 and Rock Road—and suddenly I could see it all clearly. From that moment on, I was in business with God. I let God take control. I was now seeking first the kingdom of God."

And just as Jesus promised to those who seek first the kingdom, "all these things will be given to you as well" (Matthew 6:33). I want to be clear that Steve was not seeking the secret to business success. This is not a prosperity gospel. Steve began to believe that the Bible was the best business book ever written, but not in order to make tons of money. It was a matter of living out the principles he witnessed in the life and teaching of Jesus. He made a commitment to doing business in the way of Jesus: telling the truth, loving his neighbor, glorifying God, operating with integrity, doing justice, and walking humbly before God. The old motto of "business is business" was exposed as a lie.

Through prayer and reflection, Steve was able to figure out a way to make a once-failing business profitable. He hired three coworkers and implemented the plan he had come up with. Soon he had investors, and within a short time he had ten, then fifty, then a hundred employees. He had a vision for what the work environment would be: totally equal, no offices, one big shared space. Even though Steve was the CEO, he insisted that he have the same desk and computer as everyone else. Steve is now regarded as the leading CEO in his field. All it took was an act of faith.

THE VIRTUES OF SURRENDER

Faith, hope, and love are called *theological virtues*. This is because they are built on the actions of God. The classic virtues in Greek philosophy—courage, wisdom, temperance, and justice—can be developed by a person on their own. But faith, hope, and love are entirely dependent on the action of God (grace). Faith, hope, and love are different aspects of the Christian life, derived from the good news of Jesus. (You can live an interactive life with the King in his kingdom . . . now!) Faith, hope, and love form the basis of every Christian's life, and indeed the life of the church. This big statement offers the framework for what we will explore in the next three chapters.

Faith, hope, and love are called theological virtues. *This is because they are built on the actions of God.*

What is faith? Faith is acting on what you do not know, on the basis of what you do know—but you don't really know. That may sound confusing. Let me break it down to a simple example: my schedule planner. For over fifty years I have seen the sun come up each morning. That would be over eighteen thousand times. I have known many days; therefore I believe, with Little Orphan Annie, "The sun will come out tomorrow." I don't *know* that the sun will come out tomorrow. I don't *know* that there will be a tomorrow. Rather, I *believe* there will be a tomorrow. Which is why I scheduled lunch with my friend for tomorrow.

Faith is acting on what you do not know, on the basis of what you do know—but you don't really know. Does this definition of faith make sense to you? Why or why not?

While that may seem basic, this arrangement is the basis of all faith. Faith actually increases with knowledge. We do not have faith in a person or a thing on our first encounter. I remember the first time our daughter Hope went on a date. "Do we know this guy?" I asked my wife. No, she said. "Well, we need to get to know him a bit, don't you think?" Meghan agreed. We insisted the young man come into our home and visit with us a while. Hope was not pleased. I did not grill the young man; I just asked some questions about his life, his parents, his school, his faith. He seemed like a good person. We also knew people who knew him, and they spoke well of him. Still, during the entire date I was looking at the clock. When she returned home safely, I breathed a sigh of relief.

That is a good example of faith. I was trusting in a number of factors. Hope knew him from a Christian summer camp. (He can't be too bad if he's a camper!) He seemed polite and well spoken.

People I knew and trusted (there's that word again) vouched for his character. I had reason to believe my beloved daughter was in good hands. I had faith. Not the kind of faith that goes around leaping, but enough faith to let her get into his car and go to dinner and a movie.

This is the same kind of faith that Steve demonstrated. He knew God—he was raised in the church. He knew the Bible. But he did not integrate them with his work. But when he was at that deep, dark place of despair, he followed the nudge of the Spirit. He did not take a blind leap of faith; he went on a seven-month journey to unite his head and his heart. He made a decision to do business with God and God's ways, making that his primary goal. He took what he knew (God was good; God wanted to be with him) and let God out of the box he had put God in. That was a move of faith.

BIBLICAL FAITH

One of my favorite stories in the Bible concerning faith is also a strange one. It is in Genesis 15, about the interaction of Abram (later changed to Abraham) with God regarding his calling and his future. The "word of the Lord" came to Abram in a vision. God tells Abram that God is with him, and a great future lies ahead for him. Abram reminds God that he and his wife are childless. God tells Abram to look up and count the stars. God tells Abram that his offspring will be more numerous than the stars. Then we read these famous words: "And he believed the Lord; and the Lord reckoned it to him as righteousness" (Genesis 15:6).

God's promises to Abram are not over. God then tells Abram that he will bring him to a land that he will possess. Abram asks how he will know that he shall possess it. God tells Abram to do something in order to prove his promise. God instructs Abram to find a cow, a goat, a ram, a turtledove, and a pigeon and offer them as a sacrifice. God gives Abram specific instructions: cut the animals in two (except the birds) and lay each half opposite its other half. Abram does as asked and stands guard over the offerings.

Then comes a part of the story that is easy to overlook, but it has a lot to teach: "And when birds of prey came down on the carcasses, Abram drove them away" (Genesis 15:11). Stop for a moment. Imagine this scene. Abram is shooing away the birds. Why? He is waiting. He is waiting *in faith*. He believes that God is going to act. He does not know how exactly. But God has given him instructions, and he is being obedient. He is *shooing by faith*.

When nightfall comes, a smoking fire pot and a flaming torch pass between the pieces. The story ends, "On that day the LORD made a covenant with Abram, saying, 'To your descendants I give this land'" (Genesis 15:18). It is a powerful story that frames the story of Israel. Abram would become Abraham and continue to be a person of faith. Abraham even earned the title "the father of faith." But I love the part about shooing the birds. It is a simple but beautiful act of faith.

Abraham is only one of the "great cloud of witnesses" who demonstrated faith (Hebrews 12:1). In Hebrews 11 we learn that by faith Abel offered a more acceptable sacrifice, by faith Enoch did not die but was taken away, by faith Noah warned the people of the coming doom and by faith built an ark, by faith Abraham was willing to sacrifice Isaac, by faith the prostitute Rahab was spared for harboring spies, and by faith Moses chose ill-treatment in order to be with his people, thus rejecting the pleasure of sin for a season.

By faith the Christian martyrs gave their lives rather than denounce their faith. The Bible, and all of Christian history, is filled with men and women who trusted God and acted in faith.

FAITH AS AN EXTENSION OF KNOWLEDGE

In general, faith is acting on the trust that is established by the relationship between persons or a person and a thing. As I write I am sitting on my desk chair, which I have done for over twenty years (perhaps I need a new chair). The first time I sat down on the chair, it was in the store where I bought it. I sat down gently and slowly, easing myself into the seat. Then I began to rock a bit and swivel. I spun a few circles, giving it a full test drive. It was comfortable and fit me well, so I bought it. Now, having sat in this chair thousands of times, I do not sit down gently and slowly. I flop into it. Why? I trust it. I have a long relationship with this chair. It has never let me down. I call this "chair faith."

Paul put it simply: "Faith comes from what is heard, and what is heard comes through the word of Christ" (Romans 10:17). Faith does not come out of nowhere. A word comes to us, we hear it, and we either believe it or not. Faith in God works this way: Jesus addresses us (through personal address, the Bible, a sermon, etc.), and we hear it. We then decide whether or not it is true. Truth is that which is in accord with reality, that which we can rely on. If we deem the word to be true, then we believe. Faith comes from hearing the Word of God and trusting it.

Is it possible to have faith without corresponding action?

The apostle John proclaims, "We have known and believe the love that God has for us" (1 John 4:16). On what basis does John believe God loves us? He came to *know* this love. He walked with Jesus. He saw him heal. He watched him die. He saw him alive again. Everything he knew about Jesus led him to believe this basic truth: God loves us. That is why John records Jesus' prayer to his Father: "For the words that you gave to me I have given to them, and they have *received* them and know in *truth* that I came from you; and they have *believed* that you sent me" (John 17:8, emphasis added). Reception. Truth. Belief.

John could write the most famous verse in the Bible ("For God so loved the world that he gave his only begotten Son . . .") because of what he *knew* of Jesus. That is because faith is an extension of knowledge based on knowledge. Knowledge is the basis of faith. St. Augustine believed that there can be no faith, no belief, without preceding knowledge. As we come to know God through his self-revelation, we can then come to believe in God. N. T. Wright says it well: "Faith is settled, unwavering trust in the one true God whom we have come to *know* in Jesus Christ."

To be sure, faith seeks understanding. We do not have to know everything before we can act in faith. But even the great theologian Stevie Wonder knew this truth: "When you believe in things that you don't understand, then you suffer." God, through the Spirit, reaches us and teaches us about Jesus. The more we grow in this grace and knowledge, the more able we are to act in faith. Faith is never groundless. We come to know something when we have an interactive experience with it. Until we have some knowledge, we cannot act. But once we know, we can act—in a sense *not* knowing the outcome. That is when knowledge becomes faith. Faith extends knowledge into the unknown.

What is your reaction to the statement that "faith extends knowledge into the unknown"?

DAVID'S FAITH: BUILT ON EXPERIENCE

David's battle with Goliath is one of the most well-known and beloved Bible stories. Most of us hear the story and think about the miraculous part: the little boy slays a giant. I always assumed the point of the story is that if you have courage and step out in faith, God will perform a miracle. But few people realize that this story is not about a miracle but about David's faith—which was built on knowledge. This becomes clear as we read the story.

> David said to Saul, "Let no one's heart fail because of him; your servant will go and fight with this Philistine." Saul said to David, "You are not able to go against this Philistine to fight with him; for you are just a boy, and he has been a warrior from his youth." But David said to Saul, "Your servant used to keep sheep for his father; and whenever a lion or a bear came, and took a lamb from the flock, I went after it and struck it down, rescuing the lamb from its mouth; and if it turned against me, I would catch it by the jaw, strike it down, and kill it. *Your servant has killed both lions and bears*; and this uncircumcised Philistine shall be like one of them, since he has defied the armies of the living God." David said, "The LORD, who saved me from the paw of the lion and from the paw of the bear, will save me from the hand of this Philistine." So Saul said to David, "Go, and may the LORD be with you!" (1 Samuel 17:32-37, emphasis added)

David has had many experiences of God being with him. As a shepherd he has been killing bears and lions for years. Each time, he says, the LORD was with him.

David's willingness to fight Goliath, his *faith*, was not *belief without proof*. It was *trust without reservation*. He convinced Saul with his story, and Saul said, "Go, and may the LORD be with you." There are those two crucial words: "with you." That is the essence of faith: God acting *with* us. The more we know, the more we obey, and the more we obey, the more God acts. This is not transactional, like a vending machine. It is relational. Still, the more God acts, the greater our knowledge and the greater our faith. "The basis of faith is God's revelation of himself. Faith remains subordinate to knowledge; but knowledge belongs to the substance of faith."

Many years ago I heard Billy Graham encouraging listeners to keep a prayer journal. I took him up on this, and I am glad I did. He encouraged people to write their prayers and to go back to see if or how God had answered them. I began this practice with a few principles. One was from C. S. Lewis, who once said that a person whose garden has weeds should not pray about the weeds but pull them up. In other words, if you can make the change happen yourself, then do it. But when we face situations we cannot change by direct effort, such as a loved one who is ill or a financial problem that extends beyond our resources, then we turn the matter over to God. The second principle came from Dallas Willard, who said most people's prayers are so vague they would not know if God actually answered them.

So with this in mind, I began writing prayers for things beyond my power to change, but with specific requests. Luther once said we should never prescribe how God answers our prayers (time and place and manner), so I didn't pray like this: "Lord, help my friend come to trust in you at 7 p.m. on July 5." Rather, I prayed that my friend would one day turn his life over to Jesus. I also recorded the day I prayed it. And using another piece of Willard's counsel, I prayed these prayers more than once. When a prayer was answered, I made a note of it and put a star next to the prayer. When I flip through my prayer book, I see many stars (though not on all requests). This practice has increased my confidence in prayer. One particular prayer took six years to be answered. It was the one requesting that my friend would put his confidence in Jesus. I had not seen him for years, but I saw him at a barbeque a year ago, and he was eager to tell me he had become a Christian.

Again, this is not mechanical but relational. I had been asking God to move in this person's life for many years, and I believe God acted on my request. Of course, this leaves us with another problem, namely, whether we have the power to change God's mind and actions. That is not my concern here. I have come to believe that we are called to make our requests known to God (Philippians 4:6) and to trust God to answer them as he pleases. My point here is that prayer is an act of faith, based on what we have come to know about God, and that in the process of asking and answering (or not answering) we come to a greater knowledge of God, along with a greater trust.

Without God revealing himself to us, we could never exercise faith. The incarnation of Jesus is the purest form of revelation of the nature of God: "Whoever has seen me has seen the Father" (John 14:9). The incarnation creates the possibility of faith. In encountering Christ we are confronted with the question, Who was this man? We are in the same position as the disciples. I love the interaction between Jesus and the disciples when Jesus asks them if they want to reject him and go another way: "Jesus asked the twelve, 'Do you also wish to go away?' Simon Peter answered him, 'Lord, to whom can we go? You have the words of eternal life. We have come to believe and know that you are the Holy One of God'" (John 6:67-69).

Peter knew enough about Jesus to believe that Jesus had "the words of eternal life." And in so doing, he also came to believe that Jesus was "the Holy One of God." Without the action of God, faith has no ground to stand on. But God acts, which opens the possibility of faith.

In learning to grow in grace, live from above, and learn how to hear God, we must admit that we see, hear, and believe imperfectly: "Now we see in a mirror, dimly, but then we will see face to face.

Now I know only in part; then I will know fully, even as I have been fully known" (1 Corinthians 13:12). We are all a bit like the man in Mark's Gospel who cries out to Jesus, "I believe; help my unbelief!" (Mark 9:24). Our faith, our beliefs, will always contain a mixture of faith and doubt. Remember, doubts are like ants in the pants of faith. Faith is never unqualified certainty. If it were, it would not be faith. At its best, "faith is the assurance of things hoped for, the conviction of things not seen" (Hebrews 11:1).

> *Faith is never unqualified certainty. If it were, it would not be faith.*

FAITH AND WORKS

There is an age-old debate about the relationship between faith and works. Some Christians have held the position that a person cannot be saved if there are no good works to demonstrate their faith. At the Reformation, Luther asserted the doctrine of *sola fide* (faith alone) as the only way of salvation. Luther was battling the dominant narrative of his day, the belief that the church had the power to forgive sins and dispense that forgiveness on the basis of good works and perhaps money (indulgences). Luther was right to proclaim faith as the only basis for salvation.

But the nature of faith is to act. The apostle James helps balance out Luther. He writes, "You see that faith was active along with his works, and faith was brought to completion by the works" (James 2:22). Faith finds its fulfillment in action. Faith works. It is not passive. It is revealed in action. For James, faith as merely trusting in a doctrine or confession is not salvific. Only in obedience does faith find its completion. That is why he can write, with blunt force, "Faith by itself, if it has no works, is dead" (James 2:17).

LIVING OUR FAITH DAY BY DAY

What does living with faith look like in our ordinary, everyday lives? Every day becomes an opportunity to let God out of the little religious box and to allow him to be a part of every area of our lives, which Steve's story illustrates. The best and simplest (and most difficult) way to walk in faith is to take *what I am worried about* to God. When I worry about something, it is a sure sign I have not allowed God to be a part of this area in my life. By worry I do not mean being generally cautious and concerned and doing what we can. Worry is what we do after we have done what we can.

Let's say, for example, you are concerned about finding a job. This is something we can allow God to be a part of. First, we pray. We ask God to bring people or opportunities our way. I always love Dallas Willard's definition of prayer: "Prayer is what God and I are doing together." Next, it is time to listen (what we learned in chapter three). Be all ears for God. Then, when something develops, we can act in faith by doing the right thing—doing God's will, God's way. Or let's say you are worried about your son or daughter. You can stew and worry, or you can invite God into the situation.

A couple of years ago my daughter, Hope, was going through a difficult time at school. My wife, Meghan, and I were concerned about her. I decided to turn it over to God. Within a few days of consciously inviting God to be a part of this situation, people began to offer helpful counsel to us. One friend, who is a therapist, said, "Jesus doesn't worry about our kids, so you shouldn't. Just keep praying and listening to Hope." It was great counsel. Within a few weeks things began to change for the better.

Walking in faith is a way to grow in the grace and knowledge of God, to live from above, to listen to God, and to act accordingly. The more we do this, the more comfortable we become. I pray for the day that I live free of worry, the day I am able to face challenges with faith, not fear. I am human, so I am not looking for perfection. But I am praying for progress.

At the end of the day, we can turn it over to God. We can say, "I will trust in your Word. You said not to worry. You said it would not do any good, but a lot of harm. I have come to know this. So help me to act on your words. Help me to trust and not to worry." If you do this—just this—you will be acting in faith. And the more you do it, the more you will see God at work (grace) and the more you will know about God's reliability. Faith is revealed by the ease of its working. That is why we can *relax* into faith. We don't have to fake it anymore. Faith is what we need in our everyday, present moments.

Walking in faith is a way to grow in the grace and knowledge of God, to live life from above, to listen to God, and to act accordingly.

When it comes to our future we need a different kind of faith: hope.

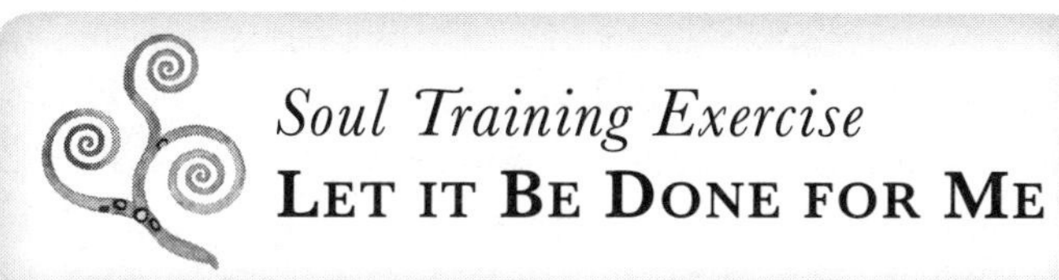

Soul Training Exercise

Let it Be Done for Me

Whoever does not come to know the face of God in contemplation will not recognize it in action.

Hans Urs von Balthasar

The practice is simple. Read a passage from the Gospels slowly, trying to see it unfold in your mind. As you read the selected passage, try to *see* what is happening in your imagination. Try to imagine the people, the places, the sights, the smells, and the sounds. Place yourself as a bystander in the story. Put all of your focus on Jesus. Notice what he says and does. Allow his personality to pulsate in every word and action. If you find something compelling in this practice, be sure to write it down in your journal.

CONTEMPLATING THE CHRIST FORM

> When he entered Capernaum, a centurion came to him, appealing to him and saying, "Lord, my servant is lying at home paralyzed, in terrible distress." And he said to him, "I will come and cure him." The centurion answered, "Lord, I am not worthy to have you come under my roof; but only speak the word, and my servant will be healed. For I also am

> a man under authority, with soldiers under me; and I say to one, 'Go,' and he goes, and to another, 'Come,' and he comes, and to my slave, 'Do this,' and the slave does it." When Jesus heard him, he was amazed and said to those who followed him, "Truly I tell you, in no one in Israel have I found such faith. I tell you, many will come from east and west and will eat with Abraham and Isaac and Jacob in the kingdom of heaven, while the heirs of the kingdom will be thrown into the outer darkness, where there will be weeping and gnashing of teeth." And to the centurion Jesus said, "Go; let it be done for you according to your faith." And the servant was healed in that hour. (Matthew 8:5-13)

FAITH PRACTICES

Prayer. Try keeping a prayer journal this week. Write your requests, being specific in what you are asking God to do, but without prescribing measure and manner or time and place, as Luther warned against.

Ask and obey. Find a quiet place to sit before God in a posture of listening. Ask God to reveal anything God would like you to do. Perhaps it is something as simple as writing a friend an encouraging note or calling to see how a friend is doing. Once you sense God encouraging you to do something, then set about doing it.

6

Embracing Hope

The best we can hope for in this life is a knothole peek at the shining realities ahead. Yet a glimpse is enough. It's enough to convince our hearts that whatever sufferings and sorrows currently assail us aren't worthy of comparison to that which waits over the horizon.

Joni Eareckson Tada

I am a fan of the Denver Broncos. I grew up in Denver and have been a fan since I was eight years old. Even though I moved away from Denver, I have a group of friends who also love the Broncos, and we watch them on TV together each week. With the advent of DVR, we are able to watch the games when we want to, not always when they air. We especially like skipping commercials so we can watch the game an hour or so after it airs. Such was the case on one spectacular Sunday in October 2011.

That year the Broncos had a young quarterback named Tim Tebow whose clean-cut image and Christian witness made him a target of media scrutiny. Tim also had a knack for the dramatic. But in this game against the Miami Dolphins (who were 0-5), Tim Tebow—and all of the Broncos—played terribly. With sad faces my friends and I watched in silence; we suffered for fifty-seven minutes of a sixty-minute game. The Broncos were down 15-0 with less than three minutes remaining in regulation. They had done nothing to offer any kind of hope that things would change.

The son-in-law of one my fellow fans, Jarrod Adams, is not a Broncos fan, so he did not watch the game with us but instead watched his team, the Dallas Cowboys, in the next room. Jarrod, however, was watching the games in real time, so he was an hour ahead of us. Jarrod walked slowly into the room of gloomy Bronco fans. I looked up to see his face. Jarrod was beaming. My first thought was, *What a jerk. He knows we are in here suffering, and he walks in with a smile?* Jarrod then said to us, "Hey fellas, mind if I watch the rest of this game with you?" He was still smiling. I once again thought bad things about Jarrod.

Then it hit me. Jarrod is one of the nicest people I know. He could never gloat over someone else's misfortune. My mind was frozen. What was he doing? Then it occurred to me: *He knows something. In fact, he must know how this ends, and he must know it is going to make us happy.* Sure enough, on the next play, the Broncos began an impressive drive that ended in a touchdown. That was soon followed by another, and with seventeen seconds to go, Tim Tebow ran the ball in for a two-point conversion, tying the game! In overtime, kicker Matt Prater (who had missed badly in previous kicks) sent the ball through the uprights from fifty-two yards out. *Broncos win*!

We went absolutely crazy, jumping and cheering like we had never done before. It was a football miracle. In fact, no team since the AFL-NFL merger in 1970 ever had been down by as many as fifteen points with less than three minutes remaining and won. It has been called the greatest three-minute comeback in NFL history. After it was over I gave Jarrod a huge hug, and thanked him for giving us hope. That is exactly what he did. He had seen the future. He knew it was good. And he let us know. That is the essence of hope.

DEFINING HOPE

Hope is a popular word. You will likely hear it many times a day. The most common use of the word is in regard to our concern about the future: *I hope it doesn't rain today. I hope we have enough money to pay the bills. I hope our team wins the championship.* Hope is concerned with the future—what will happen, be it later today, later this year, or for many years to come. When I first laid eyes on my son, Jacob, I was filled with hope for him, a long-term hope that he would have a good life. The key word is *good*. Hope longs for the good. Hope never desires a bad future.

If you listen carefully, most of the time people use the word *hope* to describe their desire for the future to be as they wish it to be. For this reason, hope, for most people, is really only *wishful thinking*. It is not grounded on any kind of certainty. Perhaps the hope is grounded in some evidence that the future might go as we want. For example, if we are planning an outdoor occasion, and we want sunshine and not rain, we may read an extended weather forecast that offers us some hope. But weather forecasts are sometimes wrong.

> *How would you define* hope *in your own words?*

This kind of hope is what can be called *natural hope*. It is based on our sheer desire and perhaps a little bit of evidence that things *might* go as we desire. For example, if I have gotten to know someone well and have developed a sense of trust in that person, my hope that they will not let me down has at least some foundation. The key word there is *know*. Knowledge is based on past experience. I do not need hope for my past (though I may need forgiveness or gratitude). I need faith in the present. Faith is based on the present. So if I know someone well (experiential, relational knowledge), I have a measure of confidence and thus can have faith this person will keep their word. And when it comes to the future, I can have some confidence that this person will continue to be reliable. This is hope.

Natural hope lacks stability and confidence. That is why superstitions are so prevalent. We think that by wearing certain socks or avoiding ladders or black cats we can control the outcome of events. On those occasions when we do (or avoid) those things, and things go well, we are quick to congratulate ourselves for wearing certain socks or running from kittens. Then we believe an illusion, thinking, *I did that*. In a world of uncertainty, anything that offers us control will do.

Many Christians do this unknowingly. They believe that by going to church, reading the Bible, or avoiding certain sins, they will be rewarded by God. This is actually a form of legalism, and legalism is mere superstition. It is the belief that we can control God by our actions. Going to church and reading the Bible *are* good, and it is wise to avoid sin—but these activities cannot control the future. They are good practices because they positively affect our hearts, souls, and minds.

Fortunately, there is another kind of hope.

SUPERNATURAL HOPE

For most of my Christian life I had natural hope. Most of my hope was wishful thinking. I trusted in the goodness of God and could quote Romans 8:28 about God working all things together for good, but in truth my hope was groundless. Only when I came to see that hope, like faith, is *based on knowledge* did I begin to experience genuine hope. This kind of hope is not natural but supernatural. It comes from living from above (eternal life in God's unshakable kingdom), from growing in *grace and knowledge*, and from hearing God and interacting with God in the present moments of my life.

Past, present, and future take on a whole new perspective when we experience eternal life. My past—and your past—have passed. They are behind us. We do not need faith or hope for our past. Our pasts are likely a mixture of things we regret, perhaps deeply, and good things we did not deserve. The magnificent story speaks to my past. The Christ event is redemptive at every turn. From Mary Magdalene to Zacchaeus, Jesus takes the broken, the sinful, and the lost and restores them. Our story is one of forgiveness. We can view our past not merely with regret but with reconciliation. Those who are in Christ need not hide or fear. Our sins cannot separate us from the love of God.

Does the difference between natural *hope and* supernatural *hope make sense to you? Why?*

In the present, we need faith. As seen in chapter five, faith is an extension of knowledge based on knowledge. We have come to know God, and because God is beautiful, good, and true, we can exercise faith in the present moment. Hope is based on the same principle. We have come to know God, and because God is beautiful, good, and true, we can exercise hope for the future. God has faithfully restored our past and is a present help in times of trouble. This kind of hope is theological hope. It is a supernatural hope.

The ancient philosophers defined what they called the *cardinal virtues*. There are four cardinal virtues: courage, wisdom, moderation, and justice. They are the basic virtues required for a virtuous life. The cardinal virtues do not require a theological or supernatural aid. Justice, for example, can exist on the natural level. People can act justly out of sheer human effort. We do not need divine intervention in order for justice to happen. The same is true of wisdom, courage, and moderation. Nonbelieving people can develop these virtues.

In contrast, the theological virtues of faith, hope, and love require divine assistance, power, and revelation. The kind of hope that we need to carry on in this magnificent journey requires a magnificent act on the part of God. We know what God has done (in the past), so we trust what God will do (in the future). Our hope is based on the promises of God. The resurrection of Jesus is the foundation of our hope. The resurrection was a supernatural act. It is not something we can do. But knowing that God has done this, we have hope that God is ultimately in control of our future. This is the kind of hope we find described in the Bible.

The kind of hope that we need to carry on in this magnificent journey requires a magnificent act on the part of God.

THE BIBLICAL WITNESS

The kind of hope we discover in the Bible is entirely based on the Christ event or the life, death, and resurrection of Jesus. If the incarnation happened, if the death of God happened, if the resurrection of Jesus from the dead happened, then the universe as we know it is completely changed. God entered our world and started a revolution. This same God defeated our two great enemies, sin and death. This same God said he would be with us always—until the end of the age. God was active in the past and is active in the present. Therefore, we can be certain that this same God will be with us in the future. Thus, hope is a theological virtue. It rests entirely on the supernatural; more specifically, it rests entirely on Jesus.

Jesus said, "Do not let your hearts be troubled. Believe in God, believe also in me" (John 14:1). The opposite of hope is anxiety. So when Jesus tells us not to let our hearts be troubled, he is calling us to hope. This is not like the hope in which we sing, like Annie, "The sun will come out tomorrow / Bet your bottom dollar that tomorrow there'll be sun." That is natural hope. Jesus is saying, "I rose from the dead. Bet your bottom dollar on me." The resurrection of Jesus is the grounds for all Christian hope.

Paul echoed the same sentiment when he told the Corinthians,

> If with merely *human hopes* I fought with wild animals at Ephesus, what would I have gained by it? If the dead are not raised,
>
> "Let us eat and drink,
> for tomorrow we die."
> (1 Corinthians 15:32, emphasis added)

Human hopes are natural hopes. If all we have is our human hopes, Paul contends, then our philosophy might as well be that of the pagans, whose slogan was "Let's party—there is nothing beyond the grave!" Paul is reminding us that Jesus' resurrection is certainly something beyond the grave, and it changes everything.

When Paul was on trial he was asked to give a defense for his gospel. He proclaimed, "I have *a hope in God*—a hope that they [the Jews] themselves also accept—that there will be a resurrection of both the righteous and the unrighteous" (Acts 24:15, emphasis added). It is hope not in humankind but in God, resting on the resurrection of Jesus in the past and looking for the resurrection in the life to come.

Peter offers the same encouragement in his first epistle: "Blessed be the God and Father of our Lord Jesus Christ! By his great mercy he has given us a new birth into a *living hope* through the resurrection of Jesus Christ from the dead" (1 Peter 1:3, emphasis added). Jesus rose from the dead *alive.* And he has remained alive ever since. The resurrection is a living hope because Jesus is forever alive. This is no mere hope in hope; it is a hope in God. As N. T. Wright notes, "Hope is settled, unwavering confidence that this God will not leave us or forsake us, but will always have more in store for us than we could ask or imagine."

The resurrection is a living hope because Jesus is forever alive.

CHRIST IN YOU: THE HOPE OF GLORY

The reality of the resurrection is also experienced in each of us who put our confidence in Jesus. We are fundamentally changed; our very being is changed by the resurrection. We are Christ-inhabited people. Paul tells the magnificent story of God's saving love story, reaching beyond the Jews to inhabit all people: "To them God chose to make known how great among the Gentiles are the riches of the glory of this mystery, which is Christ in you, the hope of glory" (Colossians 1:27). The great mystery is that Christ rose from the dead and is now, by the power of the Spirit, *in us.* And that is the hope of glory.

Earlier in that same letter, Paul tells the Colossians that the mystery of Christ within is also "the hope laid up for you in heaven" (Colossians 1:5). It is a down payment, the first fruit of what awaits us. If Christ is in us now, he reasons, then we can be sure he will be in us at our death and beyond. The grave could not stop Jesus, and the grave cannot stop Christ within us. This is all a part of the magnificent gospel. As Paul reminds them, "You have heard of this hope before in the word of the truth, the gospel" (Colossians 1:5). When Christ, who is our life, appears, we will appear with him in glory (Colossians 3:4).

Only this kind of hope, which rests not on the power of human cleverness or ingenuity or strength, but on the power of God alone, can carry us through the storms of life. Hope is certainty in a good future because of what God has done in the past. Again, Paul explains, "He who rescued us from so deadly a peril will continue to rescue us; on him we have set our hope that he will rescue us again" (2 Corinthians 1:10). Hope's unshakable confidence is based on this fact.

And yet the object of our hope remains invisible to us. That is the nature of hope. Like faith, it is unseen (Hebrew 11:1). Paul even links hope to our salvation: "In hope we were saved. Now hope that is seen is not hope. For who hopes for what is seen? But if we hope for what we do not see, we wait for it with patience" (Romans 8:24-25).

Hope is certainty in a good future because of what God has done in the past.

Notice how Paul uses two tenses: hope (future) and saved (past). We were saved by the past act of God in Christ, and now we must await the fullness of that salvation in the future life to come, which is an act of hope.

HOPE ACCORDING TO THE SAINTS

Hope has been an essential aspect of the magnificent journey from the beginning. Commenting on Romans 8:24, St. Cyprian, in the early third century, wrote:

> We do not seek glory now, in the present, but we look for future glory, as Saint Paul instructs us when he says: By hope

> we were saved. Now hope which is seen is not hope; how can a man hope for what he sees? But if we hope for what we do not see, we wait for it in patience. Patient waiting is necessary if we are to be perfected in what we have begun to be, and if we are to receive from God what we hope for and believe.

For Cyprian and others, hope is the foundation of our salvation. Hope, like faith, is unseen. We exercise faith in the present, but we rely on hope for the unseen, unknown future. This is why hope naturally creates patience.

The great thinkers in Christian history are in agreement that Christ is the foundation of hope. St. Augustine wrote, "This hope we have in Christ, for in him is fulfilled all that we hope for by his promises." Hope is Christ-centered. More specifically, it is centered, as Augustine notes, on the *promises* of Jesus. Jesus said those who keep his commandments would never taste death (John 8:52). Jesus also said, "I am the living bread that came down from heaven. Whoever eats of this bread will live forever" (John 6:51). These are promises regarding the future. And they are reliable because of the person who promised them.

Augustine went so far as to say that hope—along with faith and charity—are ways we worship God: "'Now there remain faith, hope, and charity.' These are the three virtues by which God is worshiped." To live with hope is an act of worship, giving praise to God for the unfailing confidence God has given us in Christ. Prayer too is an act of hope. St. Isaac the Syrian (seventh century) wrote, "When you pray, bring to mind the ploughman who sows in hope." To pray is to have confidence God will act in the future, just as those who plant seeds have confidence they will one day bear fruit.

St. Thomas Aquinas (thirteenth century) also wrote on the relationship between hope and prayer. He went so far as to say that hope is the key to the Lord's Prayer: "Just as our savior initiated and perfected our faith, so it was salutary that he should lead us to living hope by teaching us the prayer by which our hope is especially directed by God." When we pray each clause of the Lord's Prayer, we are doing so by hope. They are all future directed and founded on God's promises. To pray is to hope.

But we must be careful when we speak of hope, according to one of the church councils. In the Council of Trent (1545–1563) we find this word of caution: "Although all must place the firmest hope in God's help, no one must promise himself anything with absolute certainty. . . . That is, they must fear, knowing that they have been born again unto the hope of glory, but not yet unto glory." We can count on a good future, but we do not know, with certainty, exactly what it will be like. We have been given the hope of glory, but we have not yet been glorified.

When we pray each clause of the Lord's Prayer, we are doing so by hope. They are all future directed and founded on God's promises. To pray is to hope.

As with faith, there will always be a measure of doubt when it comes to hope, even this kind of hope. Perhaps you are reading this chapter and thinking, *I do not have this kind of hope*, and you might feel discouraged. As with each of these chapters, from growing in grace, to living from above, to hearing God, to walking in faith, we start where we are and ask for grace to help us cultivate hope. This book is titled *The Magnificent Journey* because living this way assumes movement and growth. We do not arrive. We will never be perfect. But we can make progress.

What has strengthened my hope is interacting with God. Mystical encounters (for example, a word from God, a timely event, an inner sense of God working with me) build my confidence in Jesus. Each day his words ring truer in my life, his resurrection seems more real in my life, and his power feels even stronger in my life. All of this contributes to my hope.

But perhaps you are currently in a place of despair. Reading this chapter may seem discouraging. I would never say to you, "Well, just be hopeful." That would be glib and trite. I have been in those places, and I remember having Christians say things they thought would be encouraging but ended up making me feel worse. Again, the main point is that hope is not something we do. Rather, it gains strength the more we begin to live from above, to grow in grace, and to walk in faith. That is all we can do in these dark valleys. I find it comforting that God is with me, even in my dark nights.

WHAT IS AT STAKE?

No more superstitions. Some Christians are inclined to treat hope as wishful thinking (*natural hope*). In so doing, we end up with superstitions and a sense of scarcity. Superstitions are ways we try to control the future. And they can be and often are religious in nature: "If I miss a church service, God will get me." Many years ago a woman in my Bible study shared with us that her father was going to have heart surgery. She told us that she prayed, "If you heal my father, I will never eat a French fry for the rest of my life." Her father came through well, and she never had a another fry.

While she meant well, this kind of behavior prevents a biblical view of hope. Superstitions are actually a form of pride. One of the primary results of genuine hope is *humility*. Instead of superstitions, such as bartering with God over fried potatoes, we stand before God in complete and utter abandonment. Christian hope is built on the work of God, the promises of God, and the goodness and power of God—not on us. Christian hope promotes humility. We come with nothing. We remain in a posture of weakness, trusting in God's power alone.

Quality of life. This kind of hope makes life worth living. Recently I preached at a church where the praise team led the congregation in the old Gaither song "Because He Lives." I had not sung it for years. But as I did, those words instilled a deep sense of hope in me.

> Because He lives, I can face tomorrow
> Because He lives, all fear is gone
> Because I know He holds the future
> And life is worth the living, just because He lives

The quality of life is impacted by the quality of our hope. It allows us to live with a magnificent optimism.

Love hopes, hope loves. Finally, this kind of hope is activated only when we enter into the bigger story. Hope is established in the larger reality going on, in the divine conspiracy that is based on love. "This hope," wrote Balthasar, "is to be clearly distinguished from purely human hope, since it cannot be described in terms of uncertainty or calculations or probability, but like faith participates in the universality of love: 'love believes all things, hopes all things' (1 Cor. 13:7)."

Faith. Hope. And love, the subject of chapter seven.

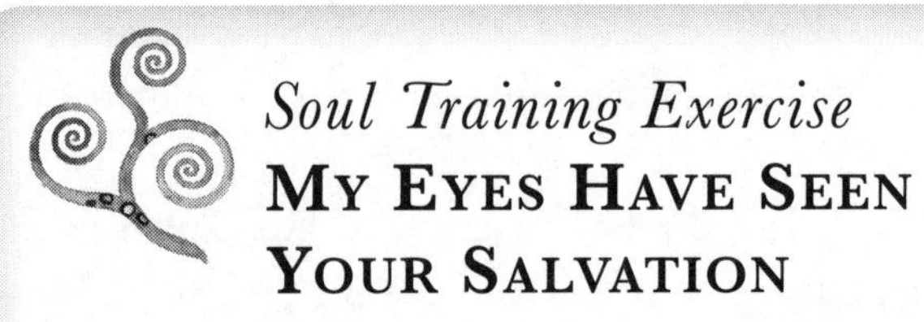

Soul Training Exercise
My Eyes Have Seen Your Salvation

The more you read the Bible, and the more you meditate upon it, the more you will be astonished with it.

Charles Spurgeon

The practice is simple. Read a passage from the Gospels slowly, trying to see it unfold in your mind. As you read the selected passage, try to *see* what is happening in your imagination. Try to imagine the people, the places, the sights, the smells, and the sounds. Place yourself as a bystander in the story. Put all of your focus on Jesus. Notice what he says and does. Allow his personality to pulsate in every word and action. If you find something compelling in this practice, be sure to write it down in your journal.

CONTEMPLATING THE CHRIST FORM

> Now there was a man in Jerusalem whose name was Simeon; this man was righteous and devout, looking forward to the consolation of Israel, and the Holy Spirit rested on him. It had been revealed to him by the Holy Spirit that he would not see death before he had seen the Lord's Messiah. Guided

by the Spirit, Simeon came into the temple; and when the parents brought in the child Jesus, to do for him what was customary under the law, Simeon took him in his arms and praised God, saying,

> "Master, now you are dismissing your servant in peace,
>   according to your word;
> for my eyes have seen your salvation,
>   which you have prepared in the presence of all peoples,
> a light for revelation to the Gentiles
>   and for glory to your people Israel."

And the child's father and mother were amazed at what was being said about him. Then Simeon blessed them and said to his mother Mary, "This child is destined for the falling and the rising of many in Israel, and to be a sign that will be opposed so that the inner thoughts of many will be revealed—and a sword will pierce your own soul too." (Luke 2:25-35)

HOPE PRACTICES

Remembering our past as we look to the future. Take time to reflect on how God has acted in your life in the past. For example, remember the times God became real in your life, perhaps those more mystical moments when you experienced the nearness of God. Pay attention to what God was doing in your life at that time, and then reflect on your future. How might God continue to make himself known to you in the days and weeks and years to come?

Redemptive remembering. Take time to reflect on your past hurts and disappointments. How was God at work in those times? How did those experiences shape who you are today?

7

Surprised by Love

My vocation is love.

St. Therese of Lisieux

I had finished a speaking engagement in Los Angeles and was waiting for my Uber car to take me to LAX. When the driver arrived, she put my bag in her trunk and I got in the back seat. "Headed to LAX. How long will it take?" I asked.

"Uh, sir, my computer says I am taking you somewhere nine minutes from here," she replied.

"There must be a mistake," I said. "I am catching a flight at LAX, and I need to get there soon."

She looked at her phone for a while, and then said, "Oh, you didn't pay for the premium ride, which allows you to have your own car. The ride you booked allows for other riders. I am picking someone up first," she explained.

"Is this person going to LAX?" I asked.

"No. I am taking them to a place thirteen minutes away. Then I will take you to the airport," she said.

I was getting angry. This was not in my plan.

Okay, time for a confession. This delay did not threaten my ability to make my flight. It would cut into the time I would have at the private airline club where I am a member. These private airport lounges offer free food and drinks in a quiet environment. I fly a lot, and because I live in a small town, I usually have layovers. So being a member of one of these clubs makes traveling a lot more enjoyable. At least that is my excuse for belonging to these clubs. Confession over.

But now it gets worse.

For the next nine minutes I thought about how inconvenient and unfair it was that I had to ride along to pick someone up and take them to their destination first. I thought it might mean I would not get my free breakfast and cappuccino! Then I noticed we were driving into a less desirable neighborhood. The driver pulled over to a modest home, and out came a young Latina woman who got into the car. She was young and pretty, with a big smile. She had just showered and her hair was still wet.

"Where are you headed?" she asked me.

"I am headed to the airport," I answered.

"Have you been on vacation here?"

"No, I was here on business. I am headed home," I said.

"Wow, do you travel a lot?" she asked.

"I do, actually."

"Wow, that must be fun. I haven't been on a plane," she confessed.

"Really? Wow. Where are you headed?" I asked.

"To my other job," she said.

"Other job?"

"Yes, I actually work two jobs. I got off of my last job at two in the morning and went home and got four hours of sleep, and now I am off to my second job. I have to work to feed my kids and my mom. She lives with us and takes care of them while I work," she explained.

I thought to myself, *Here I am, upset that I was going to have my time cut short at my private lounge, while she is happy—smiling the whole time—to go to her second job, only to follow that shift by working another job until late in the night. Rinse and repeat.* We did not take her to her workplace. We took her to a bus stop! She had to ride a bus—for who knows how long—to get to the next job. She got out of the car, looked at me with that same smile and said, "I hope you have a nice trip home. It was nice to meet you."

It is in moments like this that I realize I am not as deep in the kingdom as I want to be.

THE FOUR KINDS OF LOVE

As Therese of Lisieux says, "Love is our vocation." We were designed for love. First of all, we are made to receive love. Studies have shown that "babies who are not held and nuzzled and hugged enough will literally stop growing and—if the situation lasts long enough, even if they are receiving proper nutrition—die." One could make the case that our most pressing need as humans is to feel loved. And we are designed to give love. Performing acts of kindness and love "produces the hormone, oxytocin, in the brain and throughout the body," which leads to better cardiovascular health and slows aging.

Love is our calling. It is what we long for, what we are made for, what we are made to do. But what exactly *is* love? We use the word constantly and in many different ways. The problem is that we have only one word for love. The Greeks had four. There is *storge*, which is affectionate love, seen best in a love between a mother and a child. There is *phileo*, which is friendship love, best seen between two best friends. There is *eros*, which is sensual or sexual love, best seen between lovers. Finally, there is *agape* love, which is a love that wills the good of another without need for reciprocation. *Agape* love is not dependent on the qualities of the beloved. *Agape* love even loves the unlovely. *Agape* love can even love an enemy.

For these reasons (no need for reciprocation, not dependent on qualities or loveliness, and can be extended to enemies), Christians took *agape*, a known but not often used word, and made it their own. It was the perfect way to describe the love seen in the magnificent story. God loves the world into existence and suffers and dies for it, asking nothing in return. God's love is not dependent on our qualities. God loves us even in our sin and ugliness and rebellion. Paul states this clearly: "God proves his love for us in that while we still were sinners Christ died for us" (Romans 5:8).

Agape *love is not dependent on the qualities of the beloved.* Agape *love even loves the unlovely.* Agape *love can even love an enemy.*

The discovery that God loves us with this extraordinary kind of love started the revolution. *Agape* was elevated to the pinnacle of all loves, which it is. But in so doing, the other kinds of love, particularly *eros*, became a lesser, suspicious kind of love. Many Christians have been taught to believe that *eros* is "selfish" love and *agape* is "unselfish" love. This drove a wedge between *eros* and *agape*, and denied any relation between them. This has become the dominant way many Christians think about love. More importantly, this road more traveled affects the way they love not only their neighbor but also God and themselves.

To be sure, *eros* (as well as *phileo*) is a selfish kind of love in that it loves something about the beloved. It is dependent on the qualities of the person who is loved, whether friend or spouse. For many people, *eros* cannot lead to *agape*, nor should it. The result of this way of understanding love is that we end up believing that our love for God, self, and others should be purely *agape*. It is the best, the highest, the godliest form of love. The consequence of that is a pale kind of love for all three.

LOVE AS BOTH EROS AND AGAPE

In his masterful book *The Four Loves*, C. S. Lewis made the distinction between *need love*, which is *eros*, and *gift love*, which is *agape*. When he first began writing his great book, he believed that need love (*eros*) was a base, selfish kind of love, and that gift love (*agape*) was a selfless, higher kind of love. He changed his mind while writing, noting, "The reality is more complicated than I supposed." I suspect when Lewis dug deep to write the book, he discovered that his original narrative was too simple. In one of his poems Lewis wrote this shocking confession: "In all my life I have never had a self-less thought." We aspire to a kind of selfless love, but in truth, we never attain it. And the *eros* loves we have are not all base. My wife and I have a strong love for one another—both *eros* and *agape*—and I do not think the former is inferior. It is a wonderful part of our marriage.

The same is true of our love for God. Lewis points out that our love of God cannot help but be largely if not entirely need love. Not only do I agree, but I see this as essential, and I believe God has designed us this way. I believe it is a serious mistake—in addition to being bad theology—to "sever eros and agape into two different species." Rather, as Dr. Cynthia Bourgeault says, "*Agape is in essence transfigured desire*." How is this desire transfigured? By *kenosis*, which I define as "self-sacrifice for the good of another."

I love the great short story "The Gift of the Magi" by Ole Hallesby. It is the story of a man and a woman who are rich in love (*eros*) yet financially poor. They each give up their most precious possessions for the sake of the other. She cuts off her beautiful hair and sells it to buy a chain for his gold watch. He sells his gold watch to buy her a special comb for her beautiful hair. Were the sacrifices they made a waste? In one sense, yes. But not if love is the most important thing. Jesus' death on the cross—the highest act of kenosis—could similarly be called a waste, because many refuse to acknowledge the gift he gave. And yet we see in the cross the highest act of love.

A former student of mine, Kristen Wade, explained this combination of *eros* and *agape* in a beautiful way. She said that when she was in high school, she walked into the living room where her father was sitting. Her father said to her, unprovoked, "Kristen, I love you and always will. But I also really *like* you. I like who you are, and I like being with and talking with you." She said his words touched her in a deep way. She was not merely loved because she was his daughter. She was loved *and* liked. This is true of God toward us, and yet many of my Christian friends have trouble believing this. I admit it has been a challenge for me as well. Even after being a Christian, a minister, and a professor, I was stunned by something Brennan Manning said to me over coffee: "Jim, you don't believe God really loves you—really loves you, really likes you—not just tolerates you." I was caught off guard, but I had to admit it was true.

LOVING IN THE KINGDOM OF GOD

In Bernini's great sculpture of Teresa of Ávila, we see Teresa in a state of rapture. In fact, the sculpture is titled *Ecstasy of Saint Teresa*. An angel with a spear stands above the enraptured nun, and her face alone tells a story.

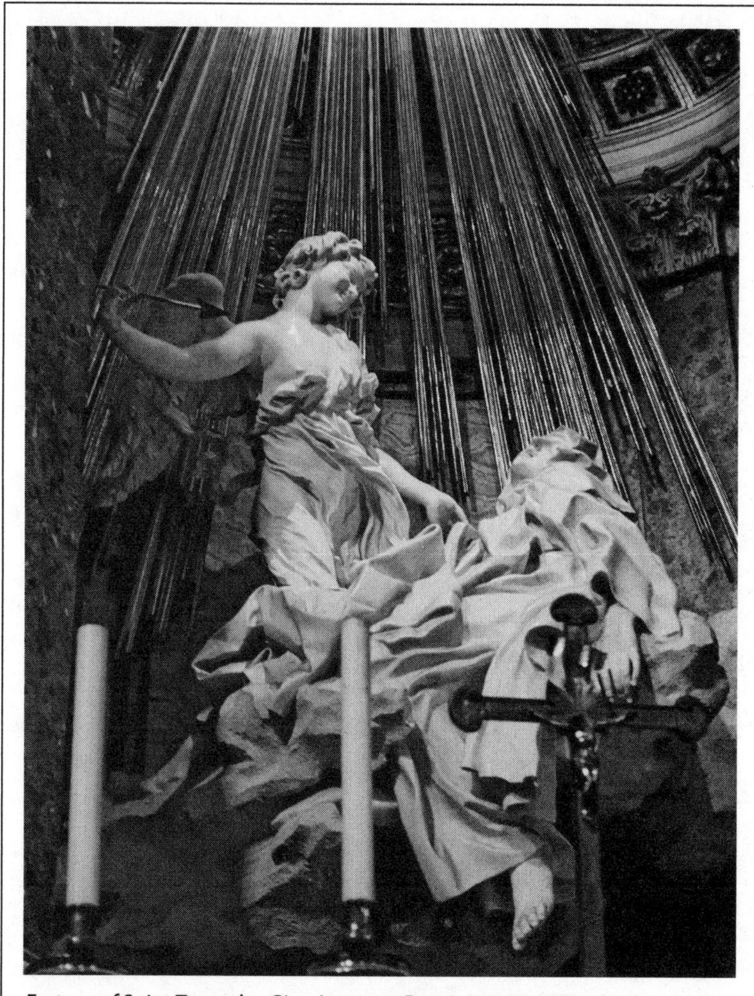

Ecstasy of Saint Teresa by Gian Lorenzo Bernini, 1647–1652

Bernini based the sculpture on a section Teresa wrote in her autobiography about a mystical encounter she had. She describes how she saw an angel, and what he did to her.

> I saw in his hand a long spear of gold, and at the iron's point there seemed to be a little fire. He appeared to me to be

> thrusting it at times into my heart, and to pierce my very entrails; when he drew it out, he seemed to draw them out also, and to leave me all on fire with a great love of God. The pain was so great, that it made me moan; and yet so surpassing was the sweetness of this excessive pain, that I could not wish to be rid of it. The soul is satisfied now with nothing less than God. The pain is not bodily, but spiritual; though the body has its share in it. It is a caressing of love so sweet which now takes place between the soul and God, that I pray God of His goodness to make him experience it who may think that I am lying.

I suspect in reading this you felt a little uneasy. We are not used to erotic language when it comes to our relationship with God. It is indeed the road less traveled.

Does the thought that God's love for you is not only agape *but* eros *make you uncomfortable? If so, why?*

What if God desired to be desired? Would that make God something less? And what if God loved us not only with *agape* love but also with *storge, phileo,* and dare I say, *eros*? If the sculpture made you uncomfortable, I suspect this notion made you even more uncomfortable. Theologian Emil Brunner, whose work I greatly admire, disagrees with me. He wrote, "If he [God] loves, his love is not *eros* but *agape*. He loves because he wants to give not to get. . . . We, as sinners, are not lovable to him." I beg to differ. I realize this is challenging to the shaming story so many Christians believe, the one that hinges on our being rotten to the core and therefore, as Brunner believes, "not lovable" to God.

I am not denying my sinfulness, my ugliness, or my selfishness (as established in the opening story). We are all in this condition.

And yet we see a great deal of the first three loves being demonstrated each day—sinners loving other sinners with *storge*, *phileo*, and *agape*. If Brunner was correct, then during every premarital counseling session it would be my responsibility to say to the couple, "You do realize your partner is unlovable, right?"

Why is it hard to believe that God actually likes us, is truly fond of us, or finds us beautiful? Jesus said to his disciples, "I do not call you servants any longer, because the servant does not know what the master is doing; but I have called you friends" (John 15:15). Friends are friends because they like each other. There is something they find lovely in their friend. I don't think Jesus was being sarcastic, as if he were actually saying, "I know friendship is built on really liking someone and wanting to be with them because you enjoy them. But you guys are lousy and awful, and I don't enjoy being with you. Still, let's be friends!"

And why is it so hard to believe that we can and ought to love God as we do our friends, family, or lovers? Must the only kind of love we have for God be a dispassionate love? I find it impossible to love God with *agape* love only. While *agape* loves without need for reciprocation, it turns out I need God's love in return. While *agape* loves the unlovely, I find God to be the loveliest thing I have ever encountered. Yes, *agape* loves without *any* lovable quality in the beloved, but I find *every quality* of God lovable. I love God as my Father, my brother, my friend, and my lover. There must be fifty ways to love my lover.

We have seen that faith and hope are theological or supernatural virtues. They require divine action to exist. I act in faith because God has proven himself worthy of my trust. I live with hope because Jesus defeated sin and death. The same is true of love. This kind of love is supernatural. It is found in the kingdom of God, the place where the least, the lost, the broken, and the sinful find welcome. This is not found in the kingdoms of this world, where fear and separation, suspicion and rejection rule. The only place where the truly sinful find welcome—and love, and being liked—is in the strong and unshakable kingdom of God.

The only place where the truly sinful find welcome—and love, and being liked—is in the strong and unshakable kingdom of God.

THE FORGOTTEN PART OF THE COMMANDMENT

Nowhere is this road less traveled—combining both need love and gift love—more important than in the last part of the second part of the greatest commandment: *loving ourselves*. My friend Joe Davis is a pastor in England. He said to me recently, "I love teaching your books in the The Good and Beautiful series. I have led hundreds of people through them, and they are so helpful. But you are missing one book: *The Good and Beautiful You*." I asked Joe why, and he said, "Everywhere I go I meet people—Christians—who despise themselves. They may be able to believe that somehow God loves them, but they cannot love themselves."

I think this can be traced to the same problem discussed earlier. When we start with the notion that we are rotten sinners who, as Brunner said, "God cannot love," how in the world can we love ourselves? Perhaps only with *agape*. God is God, so God can love with *agape*. But that is beyond me. I don't know how to love myself while seeing nothing of worth in me. The same is true of affectionate love and friendship love. I am well-acquainted with my failures. I am gifted at self-punishment. I can punish myself fifty times over one failure. So if *God* cannot find anything lovable in me, and only loves me because he is God, and if *I* cannot find anything lovable in me, is there any hope of fulfilling the commandment to love myself?

Aristotle famously said, "We ought to be our own best friend." I love that. I have been working on it for a while. Dallas Willard's simple but profound definition of love, which finds its roots in Aristotle, is this: "To love is to will and to act for the good of another." If I am to love myself, I must want and do things that do me good; I must desire my own well-being. That seems good and right. But if I do not like myself (I am no stranger to self-hatred), this will be nearly impossible. The only way to love myself is to see myself as God sees me—not as unlovable garbage but as someone God truly desires.

> *What are two or three ways you can learn to see yourself as God sees you?*

MILK AND HONEY

René Spitz conducted a fascinating study of children born and raised in prison, in difficult and unhygienic and impoverished conditions. But they were raised by their actual mothers. He compared these children to those who were raised in comfortable orphanages with hygienically impeccable conditions but *without* their mothers. They were raised under the care of trained nurses. Spitz found that in terms of mental health and physical illness, the children raised in the prisons were "far better off." Josef Pieper concludes, "They [children raised in orphanages] received plenty of 'milk'; what was lacking was—the 'honey.'" By milk he means basic provisions and care, but by honey he means "the happiness of existing." The children in the prisons were told, with or without words, How good it is that you exist. The children raised in affluence were not.

While Dallas Willard's definition stands true, I believe it provides the milk but lacks the honey. I need *agape* love. I need to be cared for, provided for. But I also need others to say to me, "How good it is that you exist." And I need to feel the same way about myself. I need more than simply willing the good for myself. I need to say to myself, "Jim, how good it is that you exist!" With an exclamation point. The more I am able to do that, the more I am able to be, as Aristotle counseled, "my best friend." The same is true of God: "How good it is that you exist, God! How very, very good." And to everyone and everything I encounter I ought to say, "How good it is that you exist!" My dog Winston is sitting by me as I write. I just told him, "Winston, how good it is that you exist." He walked over to me as if to say, "Prove it by petting me." So I did. Milk *and* honey.

I need agape *love. I need to be cared for, provided for. But I also need others to say to me, "How good it is that you exist." And I need to feel the same way about myself.*

WE COMPLETE US: PHILEO, EROS, AND AGAPE

In both *eros* and *phileo*, we experience something we need in the one we love. They are, as C. S. Lewis said, *need* loves. There is something in us that is incomplete that *eros* and *phileo* manage to complete. In the movie *Jerry Maguire*, the main character, Jerry, seems to fall in and out of love with single mom Dorothy. The movie has many memorable, quotable lines, but two of my favorite lines come near the end. Just when it looks like their romance is over, Jerry comes back, barging into Dorothy's support-group meeting and offers a speech that begins with this line: "Hello." The speech concludes with this line: "You complete me."

That is what *phileo* and *eros* do. They complete us. Without them we remain incomplete. While Jerry, who is a talker for a living, keeps on giving his speech, Dorothy tells him to stop and utters this line: "You had me at 'hello.'" Jerry had been awful to Dorothy, so when he came back he felt he needed to make amends and re-earn her love. He did not need to. He simply needed to come home or, more directly, to say hello. That is when *phileo* and *eros* merge with *agape*. We forgive, and we love despite being wronged.

I am thankful for the many people who love me. First, God's love is the central force in my life. Jesus is my friend. I love the prayer of praise from Linda Schubert, which proclaims, "Praise you, Jesus, my spouse and my Maker." I love the Father, Son, and Spirit in every possible way. In addition, my wife, Meghan, who I have been blissfully married to for twenty-eight years, loves me with all four kinds of love, as I do her. When I first met her, the only word that came to mind was another Greek phrase: *Hubba, hubba* (not a Greek word, but *eros* to be sure). Then we became friends (*phileo*). Finally, we became affectionate husband and wife (*storge*). And because we are imperfect humans, we extend a great deal of unconditional, self-sacrificing, no-need-for-reciprocating love (*agape*).

Several years ago I was sitting in my living room waiting to take Hope to softball practice. It was about 4:30 p.m., but it was a sunny summer day and the living room was full of light. Suddenly a loud sound that resembled thunder or a gunshot rang out, and a moment later my room was dark. A seventy-year-old oak tree in my neighbor's yard, which had been hit by lightning twenty years prior, had finally broken. It fell in our front yard, barely missing our roof. I went outside and was shocked to see this mammoth tree covering our yard. I went in the backyard to my shed to get a chainsaw, but it failed to start.

I then went back in the yard and looked down my street to see sixteen neighbors all walking toward our yard. They were not coming to gawk. They had gloves and tools in their hands. "We're here to help," one of them said. My eyes filled up. I knew only a few of them by name. We were not close to them, but once in a while we had a block party. What stunned me was their desire to help us in a time of need. Soon a man named Glenn walked up with a huge chainsaw and began dismantling the tree. Others grabbed branches and broken twigs, bundled them, and took them to the curb. Within an hour the yard was completely cleared. It was a little bit of *phileo* love, but mostly *agape* love. They did not *will and act for our good* with any expectation of something in return. While their act of service was the "milk" we needed, it also came with some "honey." As we laughed and shared, working side by side, I felt as if they were saying to my family and me, "We are glad you are here."

OH HOW HE LOVES US

We all know John 3:16. We all know that God loves us. But *how* does God love us? While I disagree with Emil Brunner about God loving us with *agape* only, I find Brunner's teaching about how God loves us—and what it means—to be moving and true. Brunner defines love as "being with or in real openness for the other." But we struggle to be in that condition of *real openness for the other*. Why? Our failure to love, says Brunner, comes from our inability to live fully in the present. This, he believes, is because we all suffer from a kind of depression that stems from guilt about our past and anxiety about the future:

> He [all of us] cannot free himself from his past with its guilt and remorse. And he cannot disentangle himself from his worries, anxieties and fears about the future. Therefore he has almost no present. It is as if he is not "here." He is "there"—in the past and in the future.

This is precisely where the supernatural work of Jesus makes love possible. Jesus changes our condition:

> Christ makes us free from our past by making us free from our guilt, and he does it by taking our guilt upon himself. . . . He says: "Forget about it because that is mine. I carry your past; I carry your guilt." Faith in Christ means that our past is buried in Christ under the cross. . . . Christ makes us free from our future by saying: "I am your future, therefore you need not worry; your future is secure in God's will. Your future is eternal life with God and with all of God's people. *You* need not worry about your future; your anxiety and fear can go, must go! I am your future; your future is guaranteed in me."

In so doing, writes Brunner, we are free from our past and future, and free to live in the present, where God bestows his *agape* love on us. We have faith for what Jesus did for our past (by grace) and we have hope for what Jesus will do for our future (by grace). In so doing, he concludes, "By giving us Christ's love, Christ makes us loving." We are free to be truly present with our neighbor.

This explains why *agape* love, as with faith and hope, is possible only *supernaturally*. We are all in a condition of need; we are all incomplete. Each of us is entangled in a past and future we cannot control. In order to love the unlovely, we need the supernatural grace of Jesus' forgiveness and hope. Unencumbered, we can now love with no need for completion or return. We can be present.

THE BIBLICAL WITNESS

While most people have memorized John 3:16 ("For God so loved the world . . ."), I suspect few have memorized *First* John 3:16: "We know love by this, that he laid down his life for us—and we ought to lay down our lives for one another." John continues, "How does

God's love abide in anyone who has the world's goods and sees a brother or sister in need and yet refuses help?" (1 John 3:17). The New Testament is unequivocally clear that the love of God must lead to love of neighbor and self. Jesus loved us by giving his life for us, but most of us will not have to love to that extent. John put it well: if we have and we see those who have not and refuse to give, the love of God is not in us.

Jesus was also clear about the mark of a true follower: "By this everyone will know that you are my disciples, if you have love for one another" (John 13:35). Our love for one another is a clear sign that we are living eternally: "We know that we have passed from death to life because we love one another" (1 John 3:14). The kingdom of this world is built on power and domination, on greed and competition. It is a dominion of darkness and death. But the kingdom of God, which we have been transferred into (Colossians 1:13), is built on love. It is a kingdom of life.

Perhaps nowhere in the Bible do we find more beautiful words about love than in the apostle Paul's magnificent passage in his letter to the Corinthians:

> If I speak in the tongues of mortals and of angels, but do not have love, I am a noisy gong or a clanging cymbal. And if I have prophetic powers, and understand all mysteries and all knowledge, and if I have all faith, so as to remove mountains, but do not have love, I am nothing. If I give away all my possessions, and if I hand over my body so that I may boast, but do not have love, I gain nothing. (1 Corinthians 13:1-3)

The spiritual gifts are dazzling and impressive. Faith to move mountains is awe-inspiring. Divesting all of my possessions to serve the poor is laudable. Martyrdom is the noblest act of all. But if these are not driven by love, they amount to nothing.

Jesus demonstrates the kind of love that leads to hope on nearly every page of the Gospels. Someone who does not deserve love (Zacchaeus, the woman at the well, or the Samaritan woman) receives forgiveness *and* love. In each of these cases the person who is forgiven and loved (milk and honey) resolves to change. Even the prodigal son, whose confession of wrongdoing may have been more driven by desperation than contrition, nonetheless seems on the brink of transformation. God's forgiveness now, God's *agape* love now, is the first fruit of our inheritance.

LOVE AMONG THE SAINTS

The rise of Christianity is one of the great marvels of history. Though it began with a small group of twelve people, in a few centuries it was the dominant faith of the Roman Empire. It offered none of the usual things people sought in religion. There were no gods to appease in order to find one's needs met. Most religions, and all spiritualities, offer two things: identity and power. Christianity did not offer power in the way people usually seek it. Its central message, "take up the cross," was not appealing to our usual desires. As Dietrich Bonhoeffer said bluntly, "When Christ calls a man, he bids him come and die." And it did not offer identity as most people seek it, namely, "I am an insider; I am an elite." So what drew people into this *way* of the Nazarene?

Love.

The early Christians lived in a peculiar way to the people in the Roman Empire. They forbade the ancient practice of *exposure*, letting unwanted children, usually girls, die on the side of the road. They insisted on communal provision for widows—the most disadvantaged class of people. Christian husbands were to be faithful to their wives and vice versa, and not to abandon or be cruel to them. In Christ, the distinction between male and female did not exist; neither did the distinction between master and slave. David Bentley Hart writes, "One finds nothing in pagan society remotely comparable in magnitude to the Christian willingness to provide continuously for persons in need, male and female, young and old, free and bound alike." Hart concludes with this fact: "The church became the first large, organized institution of public welfare in Western history."

Emperor Julian (reigned AD 361–363) was the last non-Christian emperor. He referred to Christians as *atheists* because they did not believe in the gods. He once remarked, "It is [the Christian's] philanthropy towards strangers, the care they take of the graves of the dead, and the affected sanctity with which they conduct their lives that have done most to spread their atheism."

Loving our neighbor—and God and ourselves—is a dangerous act. It may get us in trouble. But more likely it will spark a revolution.

Earlier, Emperor Celsus, also not a Christian, began to worry a bit about this unassuming and unimpressive religion. He saw something in the Christians that made him uneasy. Hart writes, "It is unlikely that Celsus would have thought the Christians worth his notice had he not recognized something uniquely dangerous lurking in their gospel of peace and love."

Dangerous is a strange word, but Mark Labberton uses it in the title of his excellent book *The Dangerous Act of Loving Your Neighbor.* Loving our neighbor—and God and ourselves—is a dangerous act. It may get us in trouble. But more likely it will spark a revolution, the same one that began around 6 p.m. on Good Friday, the same one still happening in our day.

WHAT IS AT STAKE?

If love is the central message of Christianity, then we need to have a full grasp of what it is and how we do it. The road more traveled, the one in which the only kind of love allowed is *agape*, will prove to be disappointing. We need the milk, but we also need the honey. Our love for God must not be merely perfunctory service but passionate fever. Many of the great thinkers in the church, such as Bernard of Clairvaux, believed that the Song of Songs is a reflection of the kind of love we ought to have for God. Wouldn't it be inspiring to see women and men aflame with love for God?

If we fail to move beyond the incomplete gospel of substitutionary atonement, we will never see Jesus as the "lover of our souls," but only as the victim for our sins. We will have no way to see ourselves as lovable, and thus loving ourselves and our neighbor will be a challenge at every turn. Wouldn't it be magnificent to see communities of Christians who greeted each other with enthusiasm, saying by word and deed, "It is great that you are here"?

LEARNING LOVE

In the opening story of this chapter, I shared my epic fail in an Uber ride. Thankfully, my journey is not over. That experience gave me a chance to reflect on my selfishness, which can become either natural or unnatural. Despite the reality check on my depth in the kingdom, I will give myself one small break. I became present to the woman in the car, not because I was so naturally concerned with others but because of her amazing smile in the midst of a challenging life. My journey is not over. The more I am able to reflect on God's provision for my past (guilt assuaged) and provision for my future (hope for the glory to come), the more I am able to trust God's provision for the present. As I do this, I am able, as Brunner stated, to be "with or in real openness for the other." Perhaps if I have a similar opportunity, I can be in a condition of *real openness* for the other. Perhaps I will *live fully in the present*, as the young woman in the car did naturally, instead of thinking about a lounge. I imagine I will get plenty of these opportunities. And so will you.

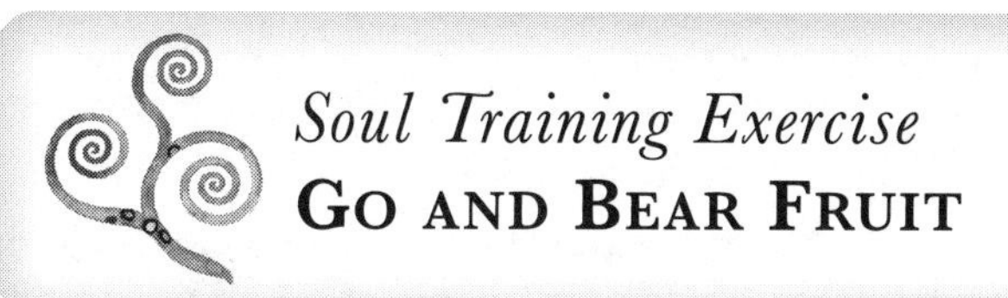

Soul Training Exercise
Go and Bear Fruit

As you read, pause frequently to meditate on the meaning of what you are reading. Absorb the Word into your system by dwelling on it, pondering it, going over it again and again in your mind, considering it from many different angles, until it becomes part of you.

Nancy Leigh DeMoss

The practice is simple. Read a passage from the Gospels slowly, trying to see it unfold in your mind. As you read the selected passage, try to *see* what is happening in your imagination. Try to imagine the people, the places, the sights, the smells, and the sounds. Place yourself as a bystander in the story. Put all of your focus on Jesus. Notice what he says and does. Allow his personality to pulsate in every word and action. If you find something compelling in this practice, be sure to write it down in your journal.

CONTEMPLATING THE CHRIST FORM

This is my commandment, that you love one another as I have loved you. No one has greater love than this, to lay down one's life for one's friends. You are my friends if you do what I

> command you. I do not call you servants any longer, because the servant does not know what the master is doing; but I have called you friends, because I have made known to you everything that I have heard from my Father. You did not choose me but I chose you. And I appointed you to go and bear fruit, fruit that will last, so that the Father will give you whatever you ask him in my name. I am giving you these commands so that you may love one another. (John 15:12-17)

LOVE PRACTICES

Each day we are given opportunities to express love. The following are simple, practical was we can do this.

- Be present with the people you meet today. This is a great but often overlooked act of love.
- Practice reflecting on your day. Ask this question at the end of your day: When today did I give and receive love or resist and withhold love?
- Notice how shame affects you. A helpful practice is first to notice when you feel shame, and then acknowledge it and turn to the face of Jesus. I find this to be a highly beneficial practice.

8

Discovering a Deeper Joy

Joy is the serious business of heaven.

C.S. Lewis

In 1988 I got my first chance to speak in front of a large audience. There were several other speakers who had written many books. Rounding out the speaker list were two rookies: me and another young guy at the time, John Ortberg. On the first day of the conference, John had given a talk on the subject of community, which was fantastic. It was funny and insightful, biblically grounded and inspiring—all the ingredients of a great talk. I was impressed. I was not surprised to see John's ministry, speaking, and writing career take off in the years to come. The following day I gave my talk and thought it went all right.

After the conference ended I saw a woman I knew standing in the hallway. She saw me and greeted me, and we hugged. I once worked in her home church for a year. I knew she had come from the East Coast to the West Coast just for this conference. She said,

"Oh, I loved your talk. It was so good." I told her thanks. Then she said, "But my, that talk by John Ortberg, that was one of the best talks I have ever heard on community. It was amazing!" I told her I agreed. Then she said, "So I went to buy a cassette tape (it was 1988 after all) of his talk, but they had long since sold out. But," she said, "I also bought a tape of your talk. They had plenty."

They had plenty.

My heart sank. For a moment I felt like a failure. For more than a moment I envied John. He had outshined me. He was the great young hope for the future, not me. I walked to the area where my ride would be picking me up. In my moment of dejection another thought came over me and I smiled. I got into the car, put down my briefcase, and sighed. My friend who was driving asked, "How are you doing, Jim?" I felt a rush of sensation I had never felt before. I started laughing and could not stop. I did not know what to call the feeling I had. But I would later discover it was one of the most important feelings we humans can have: joy. You might be thinking, *I think Jim lost his marbles and had a momentary breakdown.* I will try to show you how that moment created the opportunity for joy.

HAPPINESS AND JOY

Happiness and *joy* are often used synonymously in the Bible, as in Esther 8:16: "For the Jews it was a time of happiness and joy, gladness and honor" (NIV). Great preachers like Charles Spurgeon also used both words synonymously: "May you so come, and then may your Christian life be fraught with happiness, and overflowing with joy." While happiness and joy are quite similar, they are not the same. Happiness is tied to external circumstances. When our child wins an award, an unexpected gift is given to us, or we get a promotion at work, we feel happy. Happiness thus depends on what is *happening*. If what is *happening* is negative, we will *not* feel happy.

Joy is something much larger than happiness. Joy is not dependent on outer circumstances. Joy can be found even in the midst of discouraging circumstances. When I was told that John's tapes had sold out but mine had not, I did not feel happy. My first reaction was *unhappiness*. The external result was not what I had wanted. If the opposite had happened ("Jim, your tapes doubled in sales compared with John's"), I would have said, "Whoopee" (which is a word we use for happy feelings). I was not happy, but I did feel joy. How did I experience joy after hearing the news? For the answer we need to understand what joy is: joy is a pervasive, constant, and unending sense of well-being.

Joy flows from surrender, growing in grace, interacting with the kingdom of the heavens, communicating with God, walking in faith, living with hope, and loving God, self, and others. In other words, the first seven chapters of this book lead to joy. True joy can be experienced even in the midst of suffering and loss.

Do you agree with the statement that "Joy is a pervasive, constant, and unending sense of well-being"? Why?

In a landmark study, three psychologists found that people who had won the lottery were not significantly more joyful than people who had been paralyzed in an accident. Clearly, joy does *not* come from the outside. And that is the key. Joy comes from inside us. Our inner life, our minds and hearts, determines whether we are open to joy. In order to round out our understanding of joy, we need to have a solid, biblical understanding of the nature of joy. *Joy* is a word found frequently in the Bible and in the lives of the people in the Bible. My favorite example of biblical joy is the apostle Paul.

Paul wrote extensively about joy, especially the paradox of finding joy in suffering, which is precisely what gives joy its power.

Paul wrote about the joy of faith (Philippians 1:25), the joy of hope (1 Thessalonians 2:19), and joy in the Holy Spirit (1 Thessalonians 1:6). Most of all, Paul penned what has been called "an epistle of joy" (Philippians) while he was *in prison*! Here we find a kind of joy that Karl Barth called "the defiant Nevertheless." This is because this joy is not deterred by the things of this world. It is joy in the Lord (Philippians 4:4).

A JOYFUL SAINT

Of all the saints, perhaps none is known for being more joyful than Francis of Assisi (1181–1226). Francis was born into wealth, and as a young man was considered a lothario. He went off to war but was wounded, and in his convalescence he had a vision of Jesus. Francis left his former life of money, sex, and power, and felt called to live as a mendicant beggar in chastity. But he was a person of true joy. What Francis came to understand holds the secret to joy. It can be found in this famous "Peace Prayer," which is attributed to Francis.

> Lord, make me an instrument of Your peace.
> Where there is hatred, let me sow love;
> where there is injury, pardon;
> where there is doubt, faith;
> where there is despair, hope;
> where there is darkness, light;
> where there is sadness, joy.
> O, Divine Master, grant that I may not so much seek to be consoled as to console;
> to be understood as to understand;
> to be loved as to love;
> For it is in giving that we receive;
> it is in pardoning that we are pardoned;
> it is in dying that we are born again to eternal life.

This is such a beautiful and moving prayer. What makes it so powerful is its focus on others. The yearning to bring love and pardon and faith and hope, to give and to understand, is the secret to joy. Joy comes from self-sacrificial giving. Joy comes from what we do, as a response to what God has done. The good news is that while happiness is contingent on outer circumstances and is therefore out of our control, joy is something we can learn.

In addition to the prayer, there is a powerful story about St. Francis and the way he defined *perfect* joy. One day while walking with his friend Brother Leo, he told Leo he would give him the secret of perfect joy. Like Paul in 1 Corinthians 13, he recites all the great things that one would assume would bring perfect joy, such as speaking with the tongues of angels, making the lame walk, or giving sight to the blind; having all the knowledge and wisdom in the world; having the gift of prophecy so as to know the future. All these, Francis says, will not bring perfect joy. Finally, Brother Leo implores him to teach him what perfect joy consists of. Francis says,

> If, when we shall arrive at Saint Mary of the Angels, all drenched with rain and trembling with cold, all covered with mud and exhausted from hunger; if, when we knock at the convent-gate, the porter should come angrily and ask us who we are; if, after we have told him, "We are two of the brethren," he should answer angrily, "What ye say is not the truth; ye are but two impostors going about to deceive the world, and take away the alms of the poor; begone I say"; if then he refuse to open to us, and leave us outside, exposed to the snow and rain, suffering from cold and hunger till nightfall—then, if we accept such injustice, such cruelty and such contempt with patience, without being ruffled and without murmuring, believing with humility and charity that the porter really knows

> us, and that it is God who maketh him to speak thus against us, write down, O Brother Leo, that this is perfect joy.

Again, it is clear that joy is not based on outward circumstances. Francis is explaining that when, in the midst of suffering, we accept injustice but do not murmur and instead live with humility and charity, we will find perfect joy.

LEARNING JOY FROM A DOG

Like faith, hope, and love, joy is a *supernatural* virtue we cannot manufacture. We can only be truly joyful *in the kingdom*, because only in the kingdom do we have strength to accept injustice with patience. In the kingdom I know I am safe and secure, that I have provision and power, that I have significance and love—things the world cannot give and cannot take away. This is the same paradox Paul described when he said God's power is made perfect in our *weakness* (2 Corinthians 12:9). Living in the kingdom of God, however, requires that we surrender.

Joy begins when we enter the narrow way of Jesus, choosing to live as his apprentice, in continual surrender and reliance on Jesus. Joy continues when we grow in grace, live from above, and engage in an interactive conversation with God. Joy is also found in living by faith, hope, and love. These seven practices undergird joy, making joy possible. For example, if we do not choose the narrow way of surrender to Jesus, and remain the king or queen of our realm, it is impossible to have joy. Why? Because we were designed to live in submission to God.

The first commandment is to "have no other gods" before God (Exodus 20:3). That is the way human life is meant to thrive. To have another god (money, power, sex) before God is to have a ruined life. A dog illustrates this well.

The famous dog whisperer Cesar Millan demonstrates that a dog is wired to be under the authority of its owner and that nearly all bad behavior in dogs comes from the dog being in authority. In one episode of Millan's TV show *Dog Whisperer with Cesar Millan*, a little Chihuahua named Nunu is ruining his owner's life. The dog thinks he owns the bed, the couch, and his owner. Cesar comes in and takes authority over the dog by walking it on a leash. He brings what he calls calm, assertive energy, and the dog responds well. Cesar then teaches his owners to do the same. Within twenty minutes Nunu is calm and does not bark, bite, or claim territory. It is fascinating to watch.

The dog instinctively knows that it is not the pack leader. But when it thinks it is, the dog will misbehave. When the dog is under the authority of its owner, it becomes calm. This is much like us. We are wired to be in submission to God, to have God first in all we do. When we assert ourselves as the leader of our lives, we are going against our nature. But when we take the narrow way of surrender, putting God first, choosing to obey God's will, we are right where our souls need to be to thrive. That makes growing in grace, living from above, and listening to God possible. Faith, hope, and love can then be exercised in this relationship. Joy then becomes not only possible but inevitable.

We are wired to be in submission to God, to have God first in all we do.

FIVE PRACTICES OF HIGHLY JOYFUL PEOPLE

A part of the reason I experienced joy during the news that my tape sales were low was because I realized in that moment that what most matters is God. I did my best to glorify God, so did John, and that is what matters. The sale of tapes is inconsequential. Dallas

Willard often said that the most important thing for a person in ministry to do is to pray for the success of those we deem our competitors. I asked him why this is the *most* important thing, and he said, "Because when you can do that you are in sync with the kingdom." It was in the moment when I silently said to myself, *Good for John*, that the first stirring of joy came into my heart.

In addition to the seven basic pillars of joy already covered in this book, I believe five additional practices help build joy into our lives:

- connection
- acceptance
- reframing
- gratitude
- generosity

The following is a brief explanation of each of these practices.

Connection. The reality is this: we are all interconnected. The lie we believe most days is that we are alone, disconnected, and therefore competing for our share of the pie. When we see others as separate from us, they become a threat. When we learn to see others as connected to us, as a part of us, as interdependent, then there is no longer a threat. Now we are all allies. This is why Jesus instructed us to love our enemies. When we learn to love those we perceive as enemies, they are no longer our enemies.

I have struggled with self-centeredness. I have had to work hard (and still do) to shift my focus from myself to others. The Beatles' song "I Me Mine" is a great example of self-focus. George Harrison wrote it after the Beatles had become rich and famous, realizing that wealth and fame did not make him happy. Connection and compassion are about *we, us, ours*. When I realized that John Ortberg and I are brothers, that we are united in our faith, the joy emerged. His success is my success, just as his suffering is my suffering. Connection leads to compassion.

Acceptance. A key to joy is the acceptance of the way things are. We may not like the way things are, and we may need to work to make things different. I often think of the wisdom of the *Serenity Prayer* by Reinhold Niebuhr. Most people know the first few lines, but the full prayer is even more profound.

> God, give us grace to accept with serenity
> the things that cannot be changed
> Courage to change the things
> which should be changed,
> and the Wisdom to distinguish
> the one from the other.
>
> Living one day at a time,
> Enjoying one moment at a time,
> Accepting hardship as a pathway to peace,
> Taking, as Jesus did,
> This sinful world as it is,
> Not as I would have it,
> Trusting that You will make all things right,
> If I surrender to Your will,
> So that I may be reasonably happy in this life,
> And supremely happy with You forever in the next.
> Amen.

The opening of the prayer asks for peace, for acceptance of the things we cannot change, courage to change things we can, and wisdom to know the difference. But the last part of the prayer includes accepting hardship and trusting in God to "make all things right."

I learned this approach to life when our daughter Madeline was born with a chromosomal disorder. We had been planning for a healthy daughter and all that goes with that, such as normal growth and development, watching her one day walk and talk. We did not get that. Things did not go as we planned. Instead, we got something different. At the end of the first year of Madeline's life, someone gave us a piece written by Emily Perl Kingsley, who had a child born with autism. She compares this unexpected change of plans to having your vacation plans changed:

Why is it so difficult for us to accept the situation we find ourselves in?

> When you're going to have a baby, it's like planning a fabulous vacation trip—to Italy. You buy a bunch of guidebooks and make wonderful plans. The Coliseum. The Michelangelo David. The gondolas in Venice. You may learn some handy phrases in Italian. It's all very exciting.
>
> After months of eager anticipation, the day finally arrives. You pack your bags and off you go. Several hours later, the plane lands. The stewardess comes in and says, "Welcome to Holland." "Holland?!?" you say. "What do you mean Holland?? I signed up for Italy! I'm supposed to be in Italy. All my life I've dreamed of going to Italy."
>
> But there's been a change in the flight plan. They've landed in Holland and there you must stay. The important thing is they haven't taken you to a horrible, disgusting, filthy place full of pestilence, famine and disease. It's just a different place.
>
> So you must go out and buy new guidebooks. And you must learn a whole new language. And you will meet a whole new group of people you never would have met. It's just a different place. It's slower-paced than Italy, less flashy than Italy. But after you've been there for a while and you catch

> your breath, you look around . . . and you begin to notice Holland has windmills . . . and Holland has tulips. Holland even has Rembrandts.
>
> But everyone you know is busy coming and going from Italy . . . and they're all bragging about what a wonderful time they had there. And for the rest of your life, you will say, "Yes, that's where I was supposed to go. That's what I had planned."
>
> And the pain of that will never, ever, ever, ever go away . . . because the loss of that dream is a very, very significant loss.
>
> But . . . if you spend your life mourning the fact that you didn't get to go to Italy, you may never be free to enjoy the very special, the very lovely things . . . about Holland.

This piece captured how Meghan and I felt with Maddie. We will never get over the loss of the dreams we had for her. But there was so much about her short life that was a special blessing to us. Acceptance is essential to joy. We can either rail against the fact that things are not as we wished, or we can accept it and allow it to be reframed. You cannot reframe your situation until you accept it.

Reframing. The third joy practice is reframing. It begins by learning how to identify destructive emotions. I find the best way to get at them is to pay attention to my fears and anxieties. To be sure, God gave us fear and anxiety as means to protect us. They send an alarm that something is not as it should be. But we must not stay in that state. They actually do no good. Jesus said it best: "Can any of you by worrying add a single hour to your span of life?" (Matthew 6:27). When I feel anxiety and worry, I can reframe the situation in light of the kingdom.

A powerful example of this comes from Edith Eva Eger. She told the story of two soldiers she visited at a medical center in Fort Bliss, shared by New Mexico and Texas. Both had been badly injured in battle, and were both paraplegics. Medically, they had the same diagnosis and prognosis. One of them, Tom, was lying on his bed in a fetal position, railing against his life and bemoaning his fate. The other, Chuck, was out of his bed and in a wheelchair. Chuck explained to her that he felt he was given a second chance at life. While he was being wheeled through the garden, it dawned on Chuck that he was now closer to the flowers and could look right into his children's eyes. In the midst of a tragic situation he was able to reframe and find joy.

We accept what has happened, but then we reframe the situation looking for God to turn a curse into a blessing. For many years we had a refrigerator magnet that had a quote from Mizuta Masahide, a seventeenth-century Japanese poet and samurai (a very cool combination—poet and samurai!). The quote reads, "Barn's burnt down. Now I can see the moon."

Something bad happened (the barn burned down), but something good can come from it (now I can see the moon). Reframing allows our trauma to turn into growth, our negative events into transformation, our curses into blessings, and our sorrows into joy. It is not joy unless it can weather the storms of life.

Gratitude. The next joy practice is gratitude. There is so much to be grateful for in our lives. I have learned this through practice. My friend David Nelson made me a "gratitude tray." David is a woodworker, and he likes to make things that help people in their faith journey. The gratitude tray is a small wooden oval with two trays cut inside it. On one side there are about fifteen dried fava beans. To do this practice, I take a fava bean, hold it in my hand, and reflect on one thing I am grateful for. After a few moments, I like to say, "Thank you, Lord," and then place the bean in the empty tray. This goes on with each bean, until all the beans have been moved from one tray to the other. This can take up to a half hour. I like to do it in the morning after breakfast. I often give thanks for David, who gave me the tray, but also for the joy in his life. When I first met David he was recovering from a brain tumor that had put his life at risk. Instead of letting it bring him down, David learned that the practice of gratitude can lead to joy.

What does gratitude do for us? It changes us on every level. On the personal level, I find myself less self-centered and more spiritually minded. On the emotional level I feel more peace, less envious, and less anxious. On the physical level, I feel relaxed and less stressful. The cumulative effect of all of these is joy. I realize that the problems I have in my life should not be my primary focus. By practicing gratitude those problems are put into perspective. They seem smaller and more manageable. Instead of counting my burdens, I count my blessings, and the natural byproduct is joy.

Another helpful practice is to begin each day being grateful. Upon awakening I like to say, "I am fortunate to be alive. I have a precious life. I am not going to waste it." This shapes my attitude, even before I get out of bed. Just as acceptance means no longer fighting reality, so gratitude means *embracing* reality. There is so much to be grateful for, but gratitude is a habit that must be cultivated. I find the more I practice it, the more natural it becomes and the more it becomes my daily disposition.

> *Just as acceptance means no longer fighting reality, so gratitude means embracing reality.*

Generosity. The final joy practice is generosity. Generosity comes from a sense of plenty. I have, therefore I can give. When I feel connected, when I have accepted the things in my life I cannot change, when I have learned to reframe the events in my life, and when I live with gratitude, I find myself in a "more than enough" condition. This allows the possibility of being generous. When we give, whether time or talent or treasure, we are also in sync with the kingdom of God. We are in a position of flow. And it feels great. It leads to joy.

Our family plays touch football every year at Thanksgiving. Sometimes it can be competitive, but we have learned to tone it down, especially when the younger members of the family are playing. One of those young members of the family, Max, had been trying to play with us since he turned six. At first we could only let him hike the ball, which was not fun for him. When he turned eight, he told us at the dinner table he did not want to play this year because it was not fun. We told him to give it one more try. On the field, we encouraged Max to go out for a catch. Knowing he was young and a bit scared, we all decided (nonverbally) to let Max score a touchdown. I passed the ball to him; he caught it and began running down the field. One cousin after another dove to tackle him but missed. He ran with sheer joy, and when he got to the end zone we all clapped, and Max started screaming, "That was the greatest thing ever!" Every ten plays I would yell out, "Max play!" and everyone knew what to do. He scored four touchdowns that day, and on our way back to the house he said, "Uncle Jim, I want to play football every day."

Are you generous with what you possess? Is it easy for you to give to others? Why or why not?

It was a small gesture on our part, but it was the best part of the day for me, and actually the best football game we have ever had. Everyone had one goal—to make sure Max had fun. And in so doing, so did we. That is how generosity creates joy. Archbishop Desmond Tutu said, "Our greatest joy is when we seek to do good for others." And Jesus said, "It is more blessed to give than to receive" (Acts 20:35). It *is* more blessed to give than to receive, because one of the benefits is the joy that it brings.

WHAT IS AT STAKE?

Dallas Willard once remarked in a lecture that "joy is a great bulwark against temptation." I had sung the word *bulwark* in the great Lutheran hymn "A Mighty Fortress Is Our God," but it is not a word I ever hear. So I looked it up: "a solid wall-like structure raised for defense." What Dallas meant is that it is hard to tempt a joyful person. The joy is like a thick wall that prevents temptation from getting through. I have found this to be true. When I live deeply in the kingdom of God on this magnificent journey, I find I am joyful. And when I am joyful I am nearly invincible when it comes to sin and temptation. Sin seems silly when you are joyful. In contrast, sadness makes us vulnerable to all kinds of temptations, even those that are not appealing.

We were made for joy. It benefits every aspect of our lives, including our health and our relationships. We like to be around joyful people. I find joyful people to be infectious. I want what they have. The world is waiting to see Christians live with the joy of Jesus. Once they see it, they will want it. In addition to making our lives vibrant, joy is our most effective means of evangelism.

The world is waiting to see Christians live with the joy of Jesus. Once they see it, they will want it. In addition to making our lives vibrant, joy is our most effective means of evangelism.

Several years after the incident when John Ortberg's tapes outsold mine, I was with John as we were shooting a video. Our time to be on camera was later in the day, so John and I had time for a long, leisurely breakfast. We talked about our families, about life, and about books we were reading. At one point I told John the cassette tape story. We both laughed. Then John said, "Well, maybe that was because they thought my talk would bomb, so they only made a few. Maybe that's why they sold out so fast—there were only three!" We laughed again. There was a feeling of joy in the room.

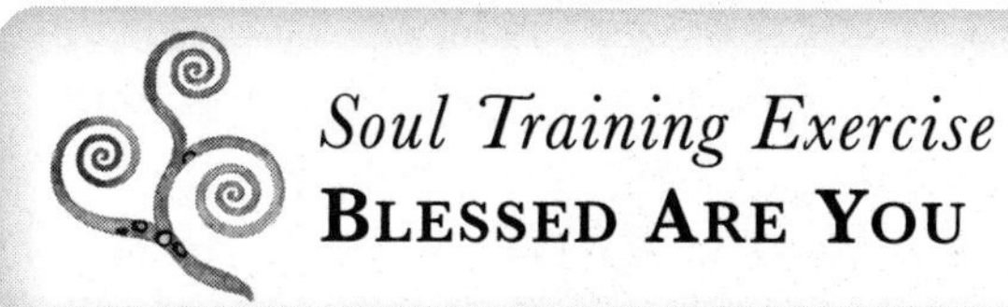

Soul Training Exercise
Blessed Are You

The Hebrew word for "meditate" means to be intense in the mind. Meditation without reading is wrong and bound to err; reading without meditation is barren and fruitless.

Thomas Watson

The practice is simple. Read a passage from the Gospels slowly, trying to see it unfold in your mind. As you read the selected passage, try to *see* what is happening in your imagination. Try to imagine the people, the places, the sights, the smells, and the sounds. Place yourself as a bystander in the story. Put all of your focus on Jesus. Notice what he says and does. Allow his personality to pulsate in every word and action. If you find something compelling in this practice, be sure to write it down in your journal.

CONTEMPLATING THE CHRIST FORM

In those days Mary set out and went with haste to a Judean town in the hill country, where she entered the house of Zechariah and greeted Elizabeth. When Elizabeth heard Mary's greeting, the child leaped in her womb. And Elizabeth was

> filled with the Holy Spirit and exclaimed with a loud cry, "Blessed are you among women, and blessed is the fruit of your womb. And why has this happened to me, that the mother of my Lord comes to me? For as soon as I heard the sound of your greeting, the child in my womb leaped for joy. And blessed is she who believed that there would be a fulfillment of what was spoken to her by the Lord." (Luke 1:39-45)

JOY PRACTICES

Gratitude tray. Try using a gratitude exercise like the one I mentioned in this chapter. You don't have to have an actual tray or dried beans. You can use any small item (marbles, beads, buttons) and two small bowls.

Ten-minute meditation on the well-being of others. Breathe in and out slowly for ten breaths. Then think of someone you know. Silently pray these prayers with each breath:

- May God bless ______________ (name of the person).
- May ________ (name of the person) be well today.
- May _______ (name of the person) find joy and peace today.

ACKNOWLEDGMENTS

I WOULD LIKE TO THANK the late Dr. Dallas Willard, to whom this book is dedicated. I was able to spend a great deal of time with Dallas, sitting under his teaching for many precious hours. The ideas in this book find their origin in Dallas's work. He first exposed me to living from above, growing in grace, walking in faith, and so on. I hope to continue his great legacy.

I also want to thank two groups of people who were willing to go through the entire book together and to provide helpful feedback and great ideas. The first group was Matt and Catherine Johnson, Tyler and Carissa Bowers, A. J. Cossell, Kristopher Swanson, Myrna Craig, Kristin Wade, Robby Rose, and Debbie Senters. The second group was from Hope Covenant Church, El Dorado, Kansas, which was led by John Carroll. It consisted of Allison Barkus, David Hinton, Shelley Reiswig, and Maddie Yager.

I also want to thank my editor, Cindy Bunch, who provided guidance and encouragement throughout the writing, as well as my agent, Kathryn Helmers, who gave me honest feedback that I needed to hear.

As always I want to thank my wife, Meghan, my son, Jacob, and my daughter, Hope, who are always a part of the writing process. Last, I want to thank my dog, Winston, who laid by my chair as I wrote, and who also provided several examples of kingdom living I used in this book. Thanks, Winnie.

Study Guide

by Matthew Johnson

CHAPTER 1: THE WAY OF SURRENDER

Gathering

This chapter introduces the importance of surrender as the entrance to living as an apprentice of Jesus. Begin your time together by sharing what comes to mind when you hear the word *surrender*. Allow these thoughts to inform you as you discuss the chapter as a group.

Exploring

1. The author opens this chapter with the story of struggling to surrender to God during a silent retreat. Can you recall a time you have surrendered to God? If so, what caused you to reach that point? How did that moment change your life? What would it mean to surrender to God each day?
2. Regarding the painting *The Annunciation* by Henry Ossawa Tanner, the author shares, "I love this painting because it is simple and ordinary." As you look at the painting, what do you notice? What, if anything, do you love about this painting?
3. Responding to Jesus' teaching from Matthew 7:13-14, Smith writes, "Stepping through the narrow gate is choosing to live as

Jesus' apprentice, to seek to obey everything he teaches." How does this understanding of being an apprentice of Jesus compare and contrast with what you have been taught previously?

4. The author explains the relationship between surrender and the magnificent journey, writing, "Surrender and obedience to Jesus is difficult. To die to oneself, to take up one's cross, is a 'hard' road but one that 'leads to life.'" It leads to "the magnificent journey of living in the unshakable kingdom of God." Have you witnessed the truth of this statement in your own journey? If so, what has it looked like?
5. Dallas Willard describes the life of nondiscipleship by what is lost: abiding peace, love, faith, hope, power, abundance of life, rest for the soul. What elements of this abundant life do you desire to increase in your own journey?

Reorienting

Scripture meditation. Each chapter's soul training exercise invites us to meditate on a Scripture passage. Chapter one suggested Luke 1:26-38 as a meditation focus. As a group, read Luke 1:26-38 aloud and then discuss the following questions.

1. As you meditated on Luke 1:26-38 what did you notice (sights, smells, sounds)?
2. Did anything spoken by Gabriel or Mary especially stand out to you? If so, what?
3. How did you feel as you stood within this story?
4. What, if anything, did you sense God was inviting you to receive or discover from this Scripture?

Surrender practices. The author offered three practices to foster surrender. They are meditating on Wesley's Covenant Prayer,

Ignatius's Suscipe Prayer, or Tanner's painting *The Annunciation*. Were you able to engage any of these practices? If so, which one? What did you discover as you spent time with this particular prayer or image? How did this surrender practice affect you?

Embarking

End your time together by reading aloud this prayer by St. Ignatius of Loyola:

> Take, O Lord, and receive my entire liberty, my memory, my understanding and my whole will. All that I am and all that I possess, Thou hast given me: I surrender it all to Thee to be disposed of according to Thy will. Give me only Thy love and Thy grace; with these I will be rich enough and will desire nothing more. Amen.

CHAPTER 2: GROWING IN GRACE AND KNOWLEDGE

Gathering

The author opens with the story of his daughter's faith in Jesus becoming her own. Spend a few minutes reflecting on and sharing your own story of discovering faith in Jesus. Keep in mind our stories can vary drastically and may be slow and subtle rather than dramatic and momentary.

Exploring

1. "*Grace* is best defined as 'God's action in our lives.' . . . I need God's grace for every aspect of my life. The air I breathe is an act of grace. The food I eat is an act of grace (which is why we say "grace" before meals). God nudges us, convicts us, comforts us, forgives us, restores us, reconciles us, and redeems us." How does this understanding of grace differ from what you

have been told? How does your understanding of grace affect your relationship with God?

2. The author makes this clarification: "Notice that when God acts, it is always *relational*. God does not act in isolation but always in relation. Therefore, these acts are known and felt in our experiences. This leads to knowledge. . . . *Knowledge* is the ability to represent something in an appropriate manner." How confident are you in your knowledge of God and the way God acts in your life? Why do you feel this way?
3. "*Faith* is the extension of knowledge based on knowledge. Because I know something (for example, that God is good and reliable), I can then act on it." In what ways might our understanding of faith change our journey with Jesus?
4. The author writes, "When we embark on this magnificent journey, we *grow in the grace and knowledge of our Lord Jesus Christ*. This is the best invitation the world has ever been given. We learn to live the *with-God* life, which is none other than living in the kingdom of God." What is helpful about this statement? What frustrates or confuses you about it?
5. The author shares the stories of Hope (his daughter), Paul, St. Augustine, and Science Mike. Each story is mystical, which the author defines as having "an element of mystery, . . . something for which words could not do justice." What is your reaction to the word *mystical*? Do these stories help you to understand what growing in grace and knowledge entails? Explain.

Reorienting

Scripture meditation. This chapter's soul training exercise invites us to meditate on a Scripture passage. As a group, read Luke 2:41-51 aloud and then discuss the following questions.

1. As you meditated on Luke 2:41-51, what did you notice (sights, smells, sounds)?
2. Did anything spoken by Mary or Jesus especially stand out to you? If so, what?
3. How did you feel as you stood within this story?
4. What, if anything, did you sense God was inviting you to receive or discover from this Scripture?

Growing in Grace exercises. One practice in this chapter was to ask Jesus to be with you as you faced a fear or anxiety. Did you have opportunities to apply this practice? If so, what did you experience?

Another practice was keeping a journal of the goodness, beauty, and truth you saw surrounding you. The author makes this connection between grace and goodness, beauty, and truth: "In the magnificent story, God is the subject of many active verbs. God *loves*, God *heals*, God *dies*, God *rises*, God *descends*, and God *ascends*—all for our benefit. Each of these acts of grace are beautiful, good, and true."

Did you keep a journal of the goodness, beauty, and truth you saw surrounding you? If so, as you review your journal, what stands out to you? What patterns do you see? How does this practice affect your relationship with and understanding of God?

Embarking

End your time together by reading aloud this Scripture and the following quote:

> This is eternal life, that they may know you, the only true God, and Jesus Christ whom you have sent. (John 17:3)

> When Jesus says . . . that eternal life is *knowing* God and himself, he is talking about having an interactive relationship

with them. When our life is caught up in God's life, our life becomes *eternal* life because it is a part of God's life.

CHAPTER 3: LIVING FROM ABOVE

Gathering

In this chapter, the author invites us to broaden our understanding of the phrase "born from above." To begin your time together, share with each other how you would have explained the phrase "born from above" to someone prior to this reading.

Exploring

1. The author begins this chapter by sharing his conversation with a couple who had lost their son to a rare disease. What was your reaction to this story? If you had been in the author's place, what would you have said to this couple?
2. Is the paradigm shift from "born again" to "born from above" challenging to you? What difference might it make in your life with God?
3. Take a moment to re-read the story from Amy Carmichael, retelling the story of young Lulla's death. How does this story make you feel?
4. Review the author's summary of the first three steps from the twelve-step program. What would it look like to apply these steps to your own life with Jesus?
5. Near the end of the chapter, the author writes, "The gospel is not merely about managing our *sin* problem, it is also about our *suffering* problem. And the good news is that we who follow Jesus have had our eyes opened wide and are living in and from another world. God is with us in our joy and our suffering. That is what the gospel of Jesus tells me." How does

this statement make you feel? How would having your eyes wide open to this gospel change your life?

Reorienting

Scripture meditation. This chapter's soul training exercise invites us to meditate on John 2:1-11, the wedding in Cana. As a group, read the passage aloud and then discuss the following questions.

1. As you meditated on John 2:1-11 in your personal devotion time, what did you notice (sights, smells, sounds)?
2. Did anything spoken by a character in the story especially stand out to you? If so, what?
3. How did you feel as you stood within this story?
4. What, if anything, did you sense God was inviting you to receive or discover from this Scripture?

Living from Above exercise. The additional practice for this chapter was an exercise in discovering the mystical in the mundane by keeping in mind the nearness of the kingdom of God as you engaged in everyday activities. How did you do with this practice? What impact did this practice have on your relationship with God? What would you do differently with this practice if you did it again?

Embarking

End your time together by reading aloud this poem by Dietrich Bonhoeffer:

Nothing can make up for the absence
of someone whom we love
and it would be wrong to find a substitute;
we simply must hold out and see it through.

That sounds very hard at first,
but at the same time it is a consolation,

for the gap, as long as it remains unfilled,
preserves the bond between us.

It is nonsense to say that God fills the gap;
God does not fill it, but on the contrary,
God keeps it empty and so helps us
to keep alive our former communion with each other,
even at the cost of great pain.

CHAPTER 4: LISTENING TO GOD

Gathering

At the beginning of chapter four the author shares a few reasons why people do not talk about their experience of hearing God. Those reasons include: it is personal; it is hard to know if it is really God; people would think we are crazy; and it makes us seem special or holy. Write these reasons on a dry erase board or large sheet of paper. Then invite the group to brainstorm other reasons. Allow this list to be a backdrop of your discussion.

Exploring

1. "Discerning God's voice is an essential part of eternal living, of living from above," writes the author. Aside from this chapter, what have you been taught about discerning God's voice? How did this chapter help your understanding of discernment?
2. Take a moment to look back over the three sections "The Biblical Witness," "Throughout History," and "Is It Really God?" These sections give examples of God speaking to people. As you look at these examples, what do you notice that you had not noticed before?
3. The author shares several ways that God speaks to him. These include: through other people; in silence; through the example

of others; and through sermons, conversations, literature, movies, and songs. Are there any examples here that you had not previously considered as ways that God speaks to us? As you consider this list, in what ways has God spoken to you?

4. The author offers three ways to test whether a word is from God: the Bible, circumstances, and another person. What is helpful about these suggestions? How have you utilized these tests in your own discernment?
5. Review the suggestions for creating the conditions for hearing God:
   - o Be willing to obey.
   - o Ask God to speak to you.
   - o Never limit how God can speak to you.
   - o Create space through silence.

Which of these steps do you find most insightful? Which one is most difficult for you?

Reorienting

Scripture meditation. This chapter's soul training exercise invites us to meditate on John 10:7-18. As a group, read the passage aloud, and then discuss the following questions.

1. As you meditated on John 10:7-18, what did you notice (sights, smells, sounds)?
2. Did anything spoken by Jesus especially stand out to you? If so, what?
3. How did you feel as you stood within this story?
4. What, if anything, did you sense God was inviting you to receive or discover from this Scripture?

Hearing practice. The additional practice for this week was to make Samuel's prayer your own. The author suggested taking a few deep breaths and then pray, "Speak, LORD, for your servant is listening" (1 Samuel 3:9). Then, with a posture of stillness and listening, be attentive to God speaking.

How did you do with this practice? Did you make any changes or modifications to the practice to help you listen for God's voice? How did this practice affect your relationship with God? Is there anything you would do differently with this practice if you did it again?

Embarking

End by reading these words about what we gain when we learn to hear God. Have the group respond to each statement with a loud "Amen!"

LEADER	As we learn to hear God, we gain an all-access pass to the kingdom of God.
ALL	**Amen!**
LEADER	Guidance and direction for the things we need.
ALL	**Amen!**
LEADER	Discernment for difficult decisions.
ALL	**Amen!**
LEADER	Character that comes as a result of obedience to the words given.
ALL	**Amen!**
LEADER	Faith, hope, and love.
ALL	**Amen and amen!**

CHAPTER 5: RELAXING INTO FAITH

Gathering

Begin your time by reading aloud twice this Dallas Willard quote. "Great faith, like great strength in general, is revealed by the *ease* of its workings. . . . Most of what we think we see as the struggle *of* faith is really the struggle to act *as if* we had faith when in fact we do not."

Exploring

1. The author gives several illustrations and analogies for faith, such as using a day planner (the sun will come up tomorrow), Hope's first date, sitting in a chair (chair faith), and Steve's journey of letting God out of the box. Which of these did you find most helpful? What was helpful about it?
2. The chapter includes two biblical stories of faith: Abraham waiting for God and David facing Goliath. What surprised you about the way faith was at work in those stories?
3. The author defines faith as "an extension of knowledge based on knowledge." How is this definition different from your understanding of faith before reading this chapter?
4. The author explains that faith, hope, and love are called theological virtues. This is because they are built on the actions of God. With this in mind, if a person asked how they could increase their faith in God, what would you counsel them to do?
5. In this chapter the author explores the relationship between faith and doubt as well as faith and works. How did his explanations of these terms address questions you have had? What questions still remain for you?

6. The author writes, "When I worry about something, it is a sure sign I have not allowed God to be a part of this area in my life." As you consider areas of worry in your life, can you see a place God is waiting to be invited into?

Reorienting

Scripture meditation. This chapter's soul training exercise invites us to meditate on Matthew 8:5-13, regarding the centurion with a paralyzed servant. As a group, read the passage aloud and then discuss the following questions.

1. As you meditated on Matthew 8:5-13, what did you notice (sights, smells, sounds)?
2. Did you find yourself in the place of a character in the story? If so, which one?
3. Did anything spoken by Jesus catch your attention?
4. How did you feel as you stood within this story?
5. What, if anything, did you sense God was inviting you to receive or discover from this Scripture?

Faith practices. This chapter's soul training exercise suggested the following practices.

1. *Prayer.* The author suggests keeping a prayer journal for one week, writing down your requests and being specific in what you are asking God to do. Have you ever kept a prayer journal in the past? How does this practice form your own faith? If you don't journal, how might this practice form your faith?
2. *Ask and obey.* This practice invites us to find a quiet place to sit before God and listen. Were you able to set aside time for such listening? If you are comfortable, share any leading you received from God. Were you able to take action on that leading?

Embarking

End your time with this prayer:

> I will trust in your word. You said not to worry. You said it would not do any good, but a lot of harm. I have come to know this. So help me to act on your words. Help me to trust and not to worry. Amen.

CHAPTER 6: EMBRACING HOPE

Gathering

The opening story involves the Denver Broncos' "football miracle" in 2011. It is a fun story of receiving hope in a small way. As a group, begin your time together by sharing times you have received hope (large or small) from someone else.

Exploring

1. In this chapter, the author continues to build on the relationship between faith, knowledge, and hope. He writes, "In the present, we need faith. . . . Faith is an extension of knowledge based on knowledge. We have come to know God, and because God is beautiful, good, and true, we can exercise faith in the present moment. Hope is based on the same principle. We have come to know God, and because God is beautiful, good, and true, we can exercise hope for the future. God has faithfully restored our past and is a present help in times of trouble." In what ways does this explanation challenge or change how you think of hope?
2. Supernatural hope is based on God's action, not our action. The author writes, "The resurrection of Jesus is the foundation of our hope. The resurrection was a supernatural act. It is not something we can do. But knowing that God has

done this, we have hope that God is ultimately in control of our future." What does it mean to you that Jesus is the foundation of our hope?

3. Consider this quote from the author, "We are fundamentally changed; our very being is changed by the resurrection. We are Christ-inhabited people." And "The great mystery is that Christ rose from the dead and is now, by the power of the Spirit, *in us*. And that is the hope of glory." How would you explain this concept using your own words?
4. The author writes, "We exercise faith in the present, but we rely on hope for the unseen, unknown future. This is why hope naturally creates patience." Do you find this statement to be true in your own experience? Please explain.
5. In considering those who may be in a place of despair, the author offers these words: "The main point is that hope is not something we do. Rather, it gains strength the more we begin to live from above, to grow in grace, and to walk in faith. That is all we can do in these dark valleys. I find it comforting that God is with me, even in my dark nights." Do you find this helpful? Why or why not? What would you add?

Reorienting

Scripture meditation. This chapter's soul training exercise invites us to meditate on Luke 2:25-35, as the child Jesus is presented in the temple and Simeon sees that he is the Messiah. As a group, read the passage aloud, then discuss the following questions.

1. As you meditated on Luke 2:25-35, what did you notice (sights, smells, sounds)?
2. Did you find yourself in the place of a character in the story? If so, which one?

3. How did you feel as you stood within this story?
4. What, if anything, did you sense God was inviting you to receive or discover from this Scripture?

Hope practices. This chapter's soul training exercise suggested the following practices.

1. *Remembering our past as we look to the future.* With this practice, the author invites us to reflect on how God has acted in our lives in the past and then reflect on how God might continue to work in our future. As you did this practice, how did it affect you? Have you ever faced difficult times by reflecting and remembering what God has done in the past?
2. *Redemptive remembering.* The second practice was to reflect on past hurts and disappointments to discern how God was at work in those times. As you looked back, did you discover anything new about God's action in your life? How did the practice impact you?

Embarking

The author points out, "When we pray each clause of the Lord's Prayer, we are doing so by hope. They are all future directed and founded on God's promises. To pray is to hope." In light of this quote, finish your time together by praying the Lord's Prayer slowly.

CHAPTER 7: SURPRISED BY LOVE

Gathering

In this chapter, the author explains the importance of being given both milk and honey. To begin your time together, affirm each other by turning to the people in your group and proclaiming: "How good it is that you exist!"

Exploring

1. The author humbly opens with a story of becoming angry during an Uber ride to the airport. What was your reaction to this story? Can you relate to the author's perspective? If so, in what ways?
2. As you looked at the photograph of Bernini's sculpture of Teresa of Ávila, and as you read the quote from Teresa's autobiography, did they make you feel uncomfortable? Why or why not?
3. The author states, "The only way to love myself is to see myself as God sees me—not as unlovable garbage but as someone God truly desires." In what ways have you learned to see yourself as God sees you? What has been the result?
4. Smith explains how *eros*, *phileo*, *storge*, and *agape* are at work in his marriage. Can you think of a relationship in your life where all four loves are present? Describe that relationship.
5. There are a multitude of statements and stories from the New Testament that affirm the author's statement that the "The New Testament is unequivocally clear that the love of God must lead to love of neighbor and self." What stories and passages come to your mind?
6. The author concludes, "If we fail to move beyond the incomplete gospel of substitutionary atonement, we will never see Jesus as the 'lover of our souls,' but only as the victim for our sins. We will have no way to see ourselves as lovable, and thus loving ourselves and our neighbor will be a challenge at every turn." In what ways has receiving God's love increased your capacity to love yourself and others?

Reorienting

Scripture meditation. This chapter's soul training exercise invites us to meditate on John 15:12-17, as Jesus commands his disciples to love one another. As a group, read the passage aloud, then discuss the following questions.

1. As you meditated on John 15:12-17, what did you notice (sights, smells, sounds)?
2. Did you find yourself in the place of a character in the story? If so, which one?
3. How did you feel as you stood within this story?
4. What, if anything, did you sense God was inviting you to receive or discover from this Scripture?

Love practices. The author offers three practices to receive God's love in our lives. The practices are (1) being present to the people you meet, (2) the prayer of examen, and (3) noticing how shame affects you.

- Which of these three practices did you utilize?
- What did you notice as you tried these practices?
- What do you sense God is inviting you to discover based on your experience?

Embarking

Conclude your time together by slowly reading this quote from Emil Brunner:

> Christ makes us free from our past by making us free from our guilt, and he does it by taking our guilt upon himself. . . . He says: "Forget about it because that is mine. I carry your past; I carry your guilt." Faith in Christ means that our past is buried in Christ under the cross. . . . Christ makes us free from our

future by saying: "I am your future, therefore you need not worry; your future is secure in God's will. Your future is eternal life with God and with all God's people. *You* need not worry about your future; your anxiety and fear can go, must go! I am your future; your future is guaranteed in me."

CHAPTER 8: DISCOVERING A DEEPER JOY

Gathering

In this chapter the author explains that happiness "is tied to external circumstances" while joy "is not dependent on outer circumstances." Spend a few minutes sharing with each other either a moment you were happy and not joyful, or a time when you were joyful and not happy.

Exploring

1. The author writes, "Joy is a pervasive, constant, and unending sense of well-being. Joy flows from surrender, growing in grace, interacting with the kingdom of the heavens, communicating with God, walking in faith, living with hope, and loving God, self, and others. In other words, the seven chapters of this book lead to joy. True joy can be experienced even in the midst of suffering and loss." In your own words, describe how the topics of this book lead to joy.
2. Pointing to the apostle Paul, the author writes, "Paul penned what has been called 'an epistle of joy' (Philippians) while he was *in prison*! Here we find a kind of joy that Karl Barth called 'the defiant Nevertheless.'" What insight do you draw from Paul's joy?
3. The author says, "Joy comes from self-sacrificial giving. Joy comes from what we do, as a response to what God has done.

The good news is that while happiness is contingent on outer circumstances and is therefore out of our control, joy is something we can learn." How has your perspective on joy changed to see it as something we can learn?

4. The five practices of joy are connection, acceptance, reframing, gratitude, and generosity. Of these five practices, which one do you feel most drawn to? How might you implement that particular practice into your everyday life?
5. Read aloud the piece by Emily Perl Kingsley. What in this essay touches you? Where are you being invited to practice acceptance in your life?
6. There is much at stake on the journey to joy. The author writes, "The world is waiting to see Christians live with the joy of Jesus. Once they see it, they will want it. In addition to making our lives vibrant, joy is our most effective means of evangelism." When has a Christian's joy drawn you toward Jesus?

Reorienting

Scripture meditation. This chapter's soul training exercise invites us to meditate on Luke 1:39-45, the story of Mary visiting Elizabeth. As a group, read the passage aloud and then discuss the following questions.

1. As you meditated on Luke 1:39-45, what did you notice (sights, smells, sounds)?
2. Did you find yourself in the place of a character in the story? If so, which one?
3. How did you feel as you stood within this story?
4. What, if anything, did you sense God was inviting you to receive or discover from this Scripture?

Joy practices. The author offers two practices to nurture joy in our lives. The practices were (1) using a gratitude tray, and (2) doing ten minutes of meditation on the well-being of others.

- Which of these two practices did you utilize?
- What did you notice as you tried these practices?
- What do you sense God is inviting you to discover based on your experience?

Embarking

Finish your time together by reading aloud this prayer, which is attributed to Francis of Assisi.

> Lord, make me an instrument of Your peace.
> Where there is hatred, let me sow love;
> where there is injury, pardon;
> where there is doubt, faith;
> where there is despair, hope;
> where there is darkness, light;
> where there is sadness, joy.
> O, Divine Master, grant that I may not so much seek to be consoled as to console;
> to be understood as to understand;
> to be loved as to love;
> For it is in giving that we receive;
> it is in pardoning that we are pardoned;
> it is in dying that we are born again to eternal life.

Notes

1 THE WAY OF SURRENDER

9 *nearer to me than I was to myself*: Augustine, *Confessions*, bk. 10. See also James B. Smith, "The Jogging Monk and the Exegesis of the Heart," *Christianity Today*, July 21, 1991.

10 *Tanner depicts Mary*: Scott Lamb, "The Annunciation by Henry Tanner," *Washington Post*, December 21, 2015.

12 *Jesus himself is the narrow gate*: Michael J. Wilkins, *Matthew*, The NIV Application Commentary (Grand Rapids: Zondervan, 2004), 322.

13 *Dallas Willard often said*: Dallas Willard, quoted in Keith Matthews, "How Is It with Your Soul?" *Sojourners*, November-December 2003, https://sojo.net/magazine/november-december-2003/how-it-your-soul.

Christian spiritual formation rests: Dallas Willard, *Renovation of the Heart* (Colorado Springs: NavPress, 2002), 64.

sickness unto death: Søren Kierkegaard, *The Sickness unto Death* (New York: Penguin, 2004).

our hearts are restless: Augustine, *Confessions*, chap. 1.

14 *the surrender of a lesser, dying self*: Willard, *Renovation of the Heart*, 68.

He is no fool: *The Journals of Jim Elliot*, ed. Elisabeth Elliot (Grand Rapids: Revell, 1978), 174.

Nondiscipleship costs abiding peace: Dallas Willard, *The Spirit of the Disciplines* (New York: HarperCollins, 1988), 263, 265.

15 *This yes is an inner assent*: Grace Adolphsen Brame, *Faith, the Yes of the Heart* (Minneapolis: Augsburg Fortress Press, 1999), 46.

18 *Surrender don't come natural*: Rich Mullins, "Hold Me, Jesus," *A Liturgy, a Legacy, and a Ragamuffin Band*, Reunion Records, 1993.

2 GROWING IN GRACE AND KNOWLEDGE

24 *When we set out*: C. S. Lewis, *Surprised by Joy: The Shape of My Early Life* (New York: Harcourt Brace Jovanovish, 1955), 200.

32 *No further would I read*: Augustine, *The Confessions of St. Augustine*, bk. 8, chap. 12, trans. Edward Pusey, Harvard Classics 2.1 (New York: Collier, 1909).

33 *The problem was that*: Mike McHargue, *Finding God in the Waves* (New York: Convergent, 2016), 124-25.

When I said the word Jesus: McHargue: *Finding God in the Waves,* 127.

3 LIVING FROM ABOVE

43 *Things above, or things of heaven*: In Jesus' day, the Jewish understanding was built on the dichotomy of "this age" and "the age to come." The age to come would appear when the Messiah would arrive and sit upon the throne ("The LORD says to my lord, 'Sit at my right hand'" [Psalm 110:1]). So, when Paul says in Colossians 3:2 that Jesus is now "seated at the right hand of God," he is claiming the age to come had arrived. But this would be mixing two metaphors: ages and planes. Paul seemed to prefer planes. For more insight see G. B. Caird, *Paul's Letters from Prison*, New Clarendon Bible (Oxford: Oxford University Press, 1976), 202.

to give Christ allegiance: Caird, *Paul's Letters from Prison*, 202.

45 *But as soon as he is born*: John Wesley, *The New Birth*, Works of John Wesley 2 (Nashville: Abingdon, 1984). I have trimmed these quotes because they were redundant and a bit long.

46 *It was in that chilly hour*: Amy Carmichael, quoted in Elizabeth Ruth Skogland, *Amma: The Life and Words of Amy Carmichael* (Eugene, OR: Wipf & Stock, 2014), 101.

47 *If a man or woman*: Julian of Norwich, *Showings*, trans. Edmund Colledge and James Wals (Mahwah, NJ: Paulist Press, 1978), 58.

50 *Nothing can make up for the absence*: Dietrich Bonhoeffer, *Letters and Papers from Prison* (New York: MacMillan, 1972), 176-77.

4 LISTENING TO GOD

54 *God talks back in a quiet voice*: Tanya Marie Luhrmann, "My Take: If You Hear God Speak Audibly, You (Usually) Aren't Crazy," *CNN*, December 29, 2012, http://religion.blogs.cnn.com/2012/12/29/my-take-if-you-hear-god-speak-audibly-you-usually-arent-crazy.

59 *He speaks, and the sound of his voice*: Charles A. Miles, "In the Garden," 1913.

66 *The inner voice of God*: E. Stanley Jones, quoted in Timothy C. Glover, "The Clarion Call of the Voice of God," FaithLife Sermons, January 26, 1997,

https://sermons.faithlife.com/sermons/111872-the-clarion-call-of-the-voice-of-god.

69 *the more silent*: William Penn, *Fruits of Solitude* (Cambridge, MA: Harvard Classics, 1909-1914).

Generally it is much more important: Dallas Willard, *Hearing God* (Downers Grove, IL: InterVarsity Press, 2012), 262.

5 RELAXING INTO FAITH

77 *Faith, hope, and love*: "Pistis," *Dictionary of New Testament Theology*, ed. Colin Brown (Grand Rapids: Zondervan, 1975), 1:601.

82 *there can be no faith, no belief*: Augustine, cited in Josef Pieper, *Faith, Hope, Love* (San Francisco: Ignatius Press, 1986), 25.

Faith is settled: N. T. Wright, *After You Believe* (New York: HarperOne, 2010), 203; emphasis added.

When you believe in things: Stevie Wonder, "Superstition," *Talking Book*, Tamla Records, 1972.

84 *The basis of faith*: Brown, "Pistis," 605.

should not pray about the weeds: C. S. Lewis, "The Efficacy of Prayer," in *The World's Last Night and Other Essays* (New York: Harvest, 2002).

prayers are so vague: Dallas Willard, "Spirituality and Ministry," Fuller Theological Seminary. I was Dallas's teaching assistant.

87 *Prayer is what God and I*: This was a phrase Dallas said many times in his lectures. I have it in my personal notes.

6 EMBRACING HOPE

97 *The sun will come out*: Andrea McArdle, "Tomorrow," *Annie*, 1977.

98 *Hope is settled*: N. T. Wright, *After You Believe* (New York: HarperOne, 2010), 203.

99 *We do not seek glory now*: Cyprian, "Cyprian of Carthage: Waiting and Patience Are Needful," *Enlarging the Heart* (blog), September 16, 2016, https://enlargingtheheart.wordpress.com/2016/09/16/cyprian-of-carthage-waiting-and-patience-are-needful-that-we-may-fulfil-that-which-we-have-begun-to-be.

100 *This hope we have in Christ*: Augustine, *Contra Faustum* 11, 7, trans. Phillip Schapff.

Now there remain faith: Augustine, *De Doctrina Christiana* 1, 35, trans. R. P. H. Green.

When you pray: Isaac the Syrian, *Ascetical Homilies*, sermon 25.

101 *Just as our savior initiated*: Thomas Aquinas, *Compendium Theologiae* 2, 3, trans. Richard J. Regan.

Although all must place: Council of Trent, session 6, chap. 13.

103 *Because He lives*: Bill Gaither, "Because He Lives," 1971.

This hope is clearly: Hans Urs von Balthasar, *Love Alone Is Credible*, trans. D. C. Schindler (San Francisco: Ignatius Press, 1963), 95.

7 SURPRISED BY LOVE

109 *babies who are not held*: Mia Szalivitz, "Touching Empathy: Lack of Physical Affection Can Actually Kill Babies," *Psychology Today*, March 1, 2010, www.psychologytoday.com/blog/born-love/201003/touching-empathy.

produces the hormone, oxytocin: David R. Hamilton, "The Five Side Effects of Kindness," *David R. Hamilton PhD* (blog), May 30, 2011, http://drdavidhamilton.com/the-5-side-effects-of-kindness.

111 *Lewis points out that*: C. S. Lewis, *The Four Loves* (San Francisco: HarperOne, 2017), 12.

Agape is in essence: Cynthia Bourgeault, *The Meaning of Mary Magdalene: Discovering the Woman at the Heart of Christianity* (Boston: Shambhala, 2010), 121-22.

I saw in his hand: Teresa of Ávila, *Autobiography*, chap. 29, pt. 17 (Mineola, NY: Dover, 2010).

113 *If he [God] loves*: Emil Brunner, *Faith, Hope, and Love* (Philadelphia: Westminster Press, 1956), 65.

117 *our own best friend*: Aristotle, *Nicomachean Ethics*, bk. 9, trans Terence Irwin.

To love is to will: Dallas Willard, from my personal notes.

far better off: "The Orphanage Problem," *National Geographic*, July 31, 2013, http://phenomena.nationalgeographic.com/2013/07/31/the-orphanage-problem. Spitz thought that infants in institutions suffered from lack of love—that they were missing important parental relationships—which in turn was hurting or even killing them. To test his theory, he compared a group of infants raised in isolated hospital cribs with those raised in a prison by their own incarcerated mothers. If the germs from being locked up with lots of people were the problem, both groups of infants should have done equally poorly. In fact, the hospitalized kids should have done better, given the attempts made at imposing sterile conditions. If love mattered, however, the prisoners' kids should prevail. Love won: 37 percent of the infants kept in the bleak hospital ward died, but there were no deaths at all among the infants raised in the prison. The incarcerated babies grew more quickly, were larger, and did better in every way Spitz could measure. The orphans who managed to survive the hospital, in contrast, were more likely to contract all types of illnesses. They were scrawny and showed obvious psychological, cognitive, and behavioral problems.

117 *They received plenty of "milk"*: Josef Pieper, *Faith, Hope, Love* (San Francisco: Ignatius Press, 1997), 175.

119 *Praise you, Jesus*: Linda Schubert, *Miracle Hour: A Method of Prayer That Will Change Your Life* (San Jose, CA: Imprimatur, 1992), 7.

120 *real openness for the other*: Brunner, *Faith, Hope, and Love*, 73.

He cannot free himself: Brunner, *Faith, Hope, and Love*, 72.

121 *Christ makes us free*: Brunner, *Faith, Hope, and Love*, 73-74.

Christ makes us loving: Brunner, *Faith, Hope, and Love*, 74.

123 *When Christ calls a man*: Dietrich Bonhoeffer, *The Cost of Discipleship* (New York: Macmillan, 1937), 7.

124 *one finds nothing in pagan society*: David Bentley Hart, *Atheist Delusions: The Christian Revolution and Its Fashionable Enemies* (Ann Arbor, MI: Sheridan Books, 2009), 163.

the church became the first: Hart, *Atheist Delusions*, 163.

It is [the Christian's] philanthropy: Flavius Claudius Julianus, quoted in Hart, *Atheist Delusions*, 154.

It is unlikely that Celsus: Hart, *Atheist Delusions*, 115.

125 *real openness for the other*: Brunner, *Faith, Hope, and Love*, 73.

8 DISCOVERING A DEEPER JOY

130 *fraught with happiness*: Charles Spurgeon, "A Happy Christian," sermon 736, *Spurgeon's Sermons* (Grand Rapids: Baker, 1996).

131 *In a landmark study*: Dalai Lama, Desmond Tutu, and Douglas Abrams, *The Book of Joy* (New York: Random House, 2016), 49. The study "Lottery Winners and Accident Victims: Is Happiness Relative?" by Philip Brickman, Dan Coates, and Ronnie Janoff-Bulman is a bit dated (1978), but I don't think the results would be different in a different decade.

132 *the defiant Nevertheless*: Karl Barth, *The Epistle to the Philippians* (Louisville, KY: Westminster John Knox, 2002), 120.

Lord, make me an instrument: While this prayer is associated with Francis of Assisi, it can be traced back no further than 1912. See "Prayer of Saint Francis," Wikipedia, https://en.wikipedia.org/wiki/Prayer_of_Saint_Francis.

133 *If, when we shall arrive*: "Perfect Joy According to St. Francis of Assisi," *Missa*, www.missa.org/joie_parfaite_e.php.

136 *Now we are all allies*: Dalai Lama, Tutu, and Abrams, *Book of Joy*, 100.

137 *God, give us grace to accept with serenity*: Reinhold Niebuhr, "The Serenity Prayer," 1943. See "The Serenity Prayer, Internet Resources," accessed May 17, 2018, http://skdesigns.com/internet/articles/prose/niebuhr/serenity_prayer.

139 *two soldiers injured in battle*: Dalai Lama, Tutu, and Abrams, *Book of Joy*, 195.

141 *gratitude means* embracing *reality*: Dalai Lama, Tutu, and Abrams, *Book of Joy*, 243.

142 *Our greatest joy is*: Dalai Lama, Tutu, and Abrams, *Book of Joy*, 59.

Under the leadership of James Bryan Smith, The Apprentice Institute (est. 2009), located at Friends University in Wichita, Kansas, provides educational experiences in the area of Christian spirituality, develops resources for individual and church renewal, and engages in research to advance the field of Christian formation.

VISION

The vision of the Apprentice Institute is the renewal of the world and the church through the formation of new people and new communities who have begun living a radical Christian life in conformity to the teachings of Jesus, as his apprentices, in the midst of the world, whether in secular or ministry positions.

PROGRAMS AND EVENTS

The following programs aid in keeping with the Apprentice Institute vision and mission:

- An undergraduate (B.A.) degree in Christian spiritual formation equipping young people to live out their faith as a follower of Jesus no matter their field of study
- A Master of Arts in Christian spiritual formation and leadership designed as a personal growth, academic and professional program (online and residency degree)
- A certificate program, titled Apprentice Experience, is a journey in discipleship intended for anyone wanting to further their study of Christian spiritual formation
- Annual national conference on Christian spiritual formation engaging leaders in the field of Christian spiritual formation

Begin—or extend—your journey of living as an apprentice of Jesus today.

For more information, go to www.apprenticeinstitute.org or email us at info@apprenticeinstitute.org.

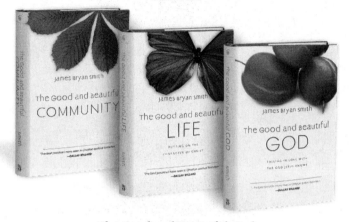

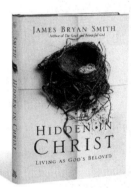

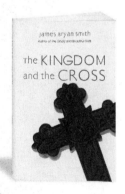

Also Available from James Bryan Smith

Formatio books from InterVarsity Press follow the rich tradition of the church in the journey of spiritual formation. These books are not merely about being informed, but about being transformed by Christ and conformed to his image. Formatio stands in InterVarsity Press's evangelical publishing tradition by integrating God's Word with spiritual practice and by prompting readers to move from inward change to outward witness. InterVarsity Press uses the chambered nautilus for Formatio, a symbol of spiritual formation because of its continual spiral journey outward as it moves from its center. We believe that each of us is made with a deep desire to be in God's presence. Formatio books help us to fulfill our deepest desires and to become our true selves in light of God's grace.